LOVE SONG
FROM BEYOND

LOVE SONG FROM BEYOND

A Voice from the Other Side

by Inga L. Chesney

A.R.E. Press • Virginia Beach • Virginia

A.R.E. Press
Sixty-Eighth & Atlantic Avenue
P.O. Box 656
Virginia Beach, VA 23451-0656

Library of Congress Cataloging-in-Publication Data
Chesney, Inga L., 1928- .
    Love song from beyond : a voice from the other side / by Inga
L. Chesney.
        p.   cm.
    ISBN 0-87604-338-4
    1. Chesney, Inga L. 2. Spiritualists—United States—Biography.
3. Chesney, Robert William, d. 1986. I. Title.
BF1283.C53A3   1995
133.9'092—dc20
[B]   95-11893

Cover design by Lightbourne Images

Dedication

To Bob: Instead of flowers on the grave

Contents

Preface

The often-used cliche "Truth is stranger than fiction" has certainly proved to be a reality in my life. It started three days after my husband's sudden, premature death. Strange and unusual things began to take place that left me wondering about the state of my mind. As I began searching for answers, I realized that what I experienced was neither hallucination nor projection born out of a possible need to avoid facing the reality of intense pain and loss, but rather a connection to the realms of the unknown.

Since I am fortunate in having a large group of caring, loving friends (some whose names have been changed in the book for reasons of privacy), it was not difficult for me to discuss the feelings of grief and pain—and with it the comforting discoveries of a new way of looking at life. In my discussions with others I found that my experience was not at all unusual. Four people out of five confessed to me, after hearing my story, that they had had a similar experience, though not necessarily to the extent of my own. It became clear to me that these matters were not discussed because of fear of ridicule.

I didn't have that problem.

I had no hesitation in sharing my experience because I trusted my sound mind, my integrity, and my sense of reality. My teen-age years growing up amidst a raging war scene taught me to face reality "as is."

Perhaps that has something to do with courage. It takes courage (and trust) to open the door to your inner life and let part of your soul be seen. Or perhaps it's just a matter of a choice of priorities: the desire to share what one considers good news and a healing factor in life for the benefit of all, against the fear of the threat of ridicule.

What happened three days after Bob died was that he talked to me—and our silent conversations continued for about eight months on a daily basis; then they gradually decreased, but occasionally take place even now.

My initial doubts were soon removed when he told me things I couldn't know concerning others, who later confirmed the accuracy of the information.

Some of the information was startling and in many ways, because of its unusual context, hard to handle. It ranged from personal to scientifically oriented matters. Since there are others involved in some of the personal data, it's easy to prove its authenticity, but the same certainly cannot apply to the scientific concepts relayed. Still, doesn't the thought, the idea, precede the search for proof?

Naturally, events of the nature described in my book prompt a certain amount of doubt in people—I was no exception. For my usually rational mind to be suddenly confronted with so many intangibles was overwhelming. Then there was the question of religious faith: Was my faith so weak that I transgressed into unacceptable, "heretical" areas?

My soul-searching brought me to the conclusion that my belief in more than one life (reincarnation) was not a transgression or lack of faith, but rather a broadening, an *extension* of it.

When recently upon the advice of a friend I bought the book *There Is a River*, the biography of Edgar Cayce by Thomas Sugrue, I was quite startled to find that—with some careful thought and deduction—the book gave me some answers to the scientifically oriented information received from Bob a few years ago.

Something about "coincidence" leaves me questioning: A stretch of many so-called "coincidences," all appearing during a certain time period and then not ever happening again, seems by logical standards and by law of percentages improbable. I no longer believe in coincidence.

Apart from all these reflections, though, one fact acceptable to everyone is that a healthy, searching mind is a fabulous tool for dealing with grief and loss. If in that process other even more rewarding and wonderful discoveries are made—who would argue with the benefit of that?

So many doors are open to humankind—if we'd just choose to walk into these as yet unexplored rooms . . .

We might find a miracle here or there.

Foreword

M y first introduction to the information, philosophy, life readings, and thoughts of Edgar Cayce took place about two decades ago. My husband and I had started exploring different concepts of thoughts and ideas. During meetings at a Special Interest Group, whose theme was that of reincarnation, we were discussing Edgar Cayce and the uniqueness of his personality, his readings, his very special gift as a true psychic. Bob and I were not immediately convinced of the reality of this gift; we thought, in the beginning, that there may have been some exaggeration.

That soon changed. The more information we gathered involving this most unusual man, the more we became convinced of his genuine and special gift. There is hardly any arguing with success!

Edgar Cayce was never a rich man. Nor was he a man of studied scientific knowledge, yet he was able, while in a sleeping state (that may be called "trance"), to diagnose and advise treatment for various ailments that proved to be correct a high percentage of the time. He had the scientific community puzzled, baffled, intrigued. Naturally there were, at first, the doubters; however, many were convinced otherwise.

But more than anything he was a *good* man.

He was a man of integrity, balance, wisdom, selflessness, compassion, and kindness. His goal was to help humanity find a better way of living, a way back to the "source"—to God. He was a devout Christian, yet respected other religions because he was able to see the connection between all that was spiritual. Perhaps this is best expressed in the words of one of his readings: "As He has given, it will ever be found that Truth—whether in this or that schism or ism or cult—is of the One source. Are there not trees of oak, of ash, of pine? There are the needs of these for meeting this or that experience. Hast thou chosen any one of these to be the *all* in thine usages in thine own life? Then, all will fill their place. Find not fault with *any*, but rather show forth as to just how good a pine, or ash, or oak, or *vine*, thou art!" (254-87)

His gift—or special ability—came to him accidentally. As a young boy with a strict father who insisted on good grades, Edgar found a way out from the pressures of study; he discovered that by placing the book from which he was to study under his head at night and sleeping on it, he would know every single word in this book by morning. When his father discovered this, he was at first very suspicious of these incidents and he showed it by even stricter examination. Soon he was convinced that his son seemed to have a most unique ability.

Edgar was fascinated by all spiritual and religious

themes. By the time he had reached his teen-age years he had read the Bible several times from cover to cover.

That was the start of a chain of events that led to what is existing now. He has been called a psychic, a seer, a mystic, a healer, a prophet. He changed the concepts of part of the medical community; he opened the minds of people to the realm of other realities. Perhaps he was to the world of psychic phenomena what Freud and Jung were to the world of psychology and psychiatry, except that he tied it all together, connected it to one. Through his special gift and his genuine, sincere, and nonprofit-seeking ability he made the world of psychic phenomena respectable and to some degree, in some circles of the scientific and medical community, acceptable. But then, what choice did they have? The actions spoke louder than words!

Life is a process of learning—ALL life, and lives.

It would be an exaggeration to say that knowing of Edgar Cayce changed my husband's and my life—but it *did* open our minds to other aspects of existence. From then on it was a slow and gradual continuing education, helped along by friends who knew more about Edgar Cayce than Bob and I did. There was Eric, Bob's best friend, who was a devout fan of the psychic; there was Doris, a nurse in a hospital where I worked, who gave me the book *The Sleeping Prophet* and who was an extremely well-read lady, who also introduced me to the works of Swedenborg and others; there were Frances and Aline, on the same "wavelength" and encouraging and nurturing esoteric thoughts and concepts in literature and experiences. It seemed as though I was being prepared for a special event.

Then, one day, that event came.

Bob, my beloved husband, died unexpectedly, without warning, of a massive heart attack.

I often wonder if I could have survived the horrible pain as well as I did had I not been so gradually and subtly introduced to all the esoteric education.

Since Edgar Cayce was a most spiritually and religious-minded man with a profound and unshakable belief in God, I felt no guilt in drawing strength and comfort from his philosophy and findings in addition to that of my Presbyterian church. As a result, I survived the tragedy of my life as a whole and healthy person. Certainly it shouldn't be surprising that an organization was founded to continue the benevolent and good work he started: the Association for Research and Enlightenment (A.R.E.), located in Virginia Beach, Virginia. It's a beautiful place, a place for spiritual renewal, tranquillity, and peace, which is visited by many people from all over the world.

Knowing of Edgar Cayce confirmed my belief in the biblical quote: " . . . faith is the substance of things hoped for, the evidence of things not seen." (Hewbrews 11:1)

1

A Hint of Symphonies

"This is the way the world ends,
Not with a bang but a whimper . . . "
—T. S. Eliot

This quote by T. S. Eliot from "The Hollow Man" keeps running through my mind for some reason.

It wasn't exactly a whimper that threw me into shock. A few days ago my world ended, and the events following have had an impact of major proportions on me. There was his voice again, making me believe that perhaps what I had heard Bob say to me on Wednesday may have been quite real. But how could that be?

A few days ago, on Monday in the early morning hours, he had died.

Without warning, after going to bed, and within a few seconds, a massive heart attack took away what was my life's meaning, made it disappear into nothing ... Or did it?

I remember sitting on the living-room floor waiting to go to the funeral parlor for the "viewing." I was dreading this day. How can I face all these people, talk normally and sensibly, and function like any other normal human being? When all I want is to die? When my only desire is to be where he is now? When I am so tired of the pain ravaging my entire body and soul? The mere thought nauseates me.

Then I heard his voice, wrapping itself around me like a soothing, healing ointment; with that loving timber which had become so familiar to me: "Honey, don't do this to yourself. I'm still here. I can do much more for you now, here, where I am. Look, remember how I always tried to do psychokinetics? Well, I can do it now! I'm having a ball!"

I couldn't help but smile at the memory of him sitting at the dining-room table: one flash of a thousand memories. He was concentrating so hard on trying to move an object with the power of his mind that the veins at his temples showed, until he eventually perspired from the effort. Then in a fit of anger at the unsuccessful attempt, he swept the innocent and now abused object from the table in utter contempt—as though *it* were at fault, and not he or his mind. "I just couldn't concentrate tonight," he muttered half in disgust, half in embarrassment.

"Mom, are you all right?" Gloria's soft, moist brown eyes had looked at me with puzzled concern. It would have to seem strange to her to see me smile on a day like this, knowing how much I loved him, how much he meant to me. "We have to go. I'm sorry, but it's time." I was grateful for—and to—my loving daughter.

"Yes, honey. I'm all right." But I didn't tell her what I had just heard. She may get even more concerned, thinking I was losing my mind.

Time, she had said.

Time alone. Time to think. Alone. Time? What *is* time? What is life? Life is a drop in a bucket, a mere sprinkle of joy and pain, interspersed with events of importance or non-importance. A collection of short stories: drama and humor, printed sometimes in red, sometimes in black, and sometimes in all the colors of the rainbow; read, and put aside, and forgotten.

But I wouldn't forget *him*. Not ever. He *was* my life.

O God—I don't want to go. If I want to go anywhere at all, it's out of this life. Into another, perhaps.

On the way to the funeral parlor the car radio played, "We strolled the rain together, laughed at the rain together . . ." I bit my lips, trying to suppress the tears. Gloria looked over at me and turned the radio off.

I recalled what I had heard. Was it real? Is there, after all, such a thing as life after death? Bob and I had discussed these issues many times during our marriage. Bob loved to debate, and he had found a willing partner in me. Somehow we had been able to find a like-minded circle of friends.

What if what I had heard was real? The thought had overwhelmed me. Caution—I warned myself—don't get carried away. Our emotions can let our minds play tricks on us. But hearing him had felt so good. It had been healing, a pacifier.

Well, I'll continue that thought some other time. Not now. Bob is dead. He died three days ago. Life will never be the same again.

Somehow I got through the day.

At home again, trying to wash my hands, I had forgotten how to turn the water faucet on. It took me a few minutes, then I remembered.

Today three of my friends have come to visit, to comfort me, to console. They've brought some food. I'm deeply touched by and grateful for their caring, though I'm not at all hungry. When I'm alone, I can't eat. But since I'm hardly ever alone, I do eat some food, sometimes.

Perhaps it's the conversation with my friends Doris, Frances, and Aline that has created the desire within me to try communication with the unknown, but wished-for contact.

The conversation had centered around political issues in world events, the concepts of Edgar Cayce, the so-called "alpha-waves," and other related matters. It was certainly a generous attempt at diverting me, and for most of the time it worked, but there have been numerous internal interruptions of pain. Each time that happened I tried to console myself with the thought of the occurrence of hearing Bob's voice a few days ago. I also remembered my doubts.

I have to be sure.

Is it possible to "be sure"?

While I'm busy making coffee in the kitchen, I hold a silent conversation within myself. Perhaps, if I try hard enough and ask a question, I will get an answer. It would be interesting to find out what I would hear. It would be reasonably clear to detect from the answer whether it has come from my own thought process or from some other source.

"Well, Bob," I ask, "if you are where I think you are, have you had any contact with the other souls around you?"

"Yes," comes the answer, "but they are far away in the distance. They're busy."

"Busy—doing *what?*"

"Re-evaluating."

"Re-evaluating what?"

While my hands are automatically handling the coffee-making procedure, I'm totally immersed in this conversation. The answer that comes hits me with such surprise that I disconnect all communication.

"Symphonies," it says.

Symphonies?!

That is utterly ridiculous. Symphonies! Perhaps I *am* losing my mind and should get myself into some psychiatric therapy. After all, it wouldn't be the first time that people who had experienced a great and traumatic loss found themselves in need of some counseling. I'm only glad that no one else knows about my attempt.

Trying not to let my experience and the puzzled shock it has created within me show, I walk my coffee pot into the living room. No one seems to notice my trembling hands.

Symphonies . . . What an odd answer. Am I really losing my mind? Suppose, though, I'm not hallucinating; what could it mean? Perhaps, after my friends leave, I should look up the word *symphonies* in the dictionary.

As soon as they leave, I grab the book. When I read the explanations for the word *symphony*, my outlook on this whole matter changes.

It says: "Symphony: an elaborate instrumental composition," etc.; an explanatory array of different meanings. Then, as I read on, it hits me: "anything characterized by a harmonious combination of elements and especially an effective combination of colors." Another one says: "harmony of sounds." Wouldn't that be applicable to the appearance, the functioning of the Universe—at least to some degree? Could it mean that our earth with all inhabitants and perhaps even other planetary systems are subject to change, slow but steady at times or very quickly at other times, from the influence of either harmonious or disharmonious vibrations? What about the expression "music of the spheres"? What about the philosopher Walter Russell's explanation of the universe: "Rhythmic balanced interchange"? Does all of this fit into the category of a "symphony"? And if it *does*—would departed souls have some influence on that "rhythmic balanced interchange"? And in which way, to what degree? Many questions without answers. What a fool I had been to disrupt the conversation! Will I ever be able to get it back? Would I *want* to? After all, there may be some dangers involved with that sort of communication.

Still, it would be worth trying. Or perhaps it would appear without any effort on my part?

I am totally fascinated and puzzled. Am I projecting a voice I'm desperately trying to hear? Or have I been tuned in to something from another dimension? Is Bob trying to help me cope by giving my mind a challenge?

That would be just like him—*if* there is such a thing as life after death. I cannot help but immerse myself in the memories of our first days together, getting to know each other. We had met over dinner with friends.

He had frequently looked at me from across the room, and while at first I was flattered to have drawn the attention of a very good-looking man, I soon began to feel a more special kind of attraction. I'm still not sure what that initial attraction was, but it wasn't too long before we were involved in a prolonged conversation.

As he was telling me about his life, I had the opportunity to study his face. Wavy, dark brown hair, cut rather short, complemented the gray eyes and rugged facial features. There was a small scar midway on his upper lip, and I couldn't help wondering how it got there. Although his body-build was strong, he didn't seem an aggressive type. His eyes radiated not only intelligence, but also the kind of quiet, gentle intelligence that had always had a strong appeal to me.

His nose was rather full—had it been more slender he would have reminded me very much of a Roman soldier. His interest in the Roman Empire, ancient Egypt, the Mayan culture, and all ancient and also fairly recent history came across to a receptive conversation partner in no uncertain ways. He seemed to know much about everything—and that made me just a bit suspicious. Perhaps that was part of my initial fascination for him. I wondered if he were for real. Could anyone know that much about so many things? But the first evening I visited him at his home, I found that I really didn't care whether his knowledge was just "bragging" or genuine knowledge. His warm and caring personality, his keen, lively, open mind with an insatiable curiosity to learn all about everything, his sense of humor—it all made me feel that I was lucky to know him.

Perhaps it was "love at first sight," but it wasn't what I always understood to be such an emotion. That "fireworks" and "seeing stars" feeling was replaced by a feeling of contentment, being comfortable, being "at home, at last." It was tranquil happiness.

I was rather shocked at this discovery. I, with my two children, had just separated from my husband of fourteen years, of which the last seven years were a struggle to keep the marriage going. I wasn't at all ready to enter into a new relationship.

With an onslaught of painful stabs into my heart, the memory of that first evening awakens me once again to reality. I can feel the cold air embracing us as we were sitting outside, huddled in warm blankets on that cold winter day, letting the clear starlight invade our senses: soothing, caressing, teasing our minds into exploration. I can still see the darkly embossed outline of the old fir trees silhouetted against that softly illuminated evening skyline, slightly swaying like reluctant, shy dancers in an unknown world.

We held each other, and we knew we belonged together. And now?

The treasures I once knew . . .

Loss. Emptiness.

Pain wants to wrap itself around my heart like a vice gripping an inanimate object.

Hansi, our German shepherd dog, diverts me by jumping up at me with demanding enthusiasm. It's time for his evening walk. With tired reluctance I comply, take his leash, and tell myself that perhaps it would be wise for me to stay down to earth and forget these thoughts of communicating with someone who's dead—the reality of my loss together with the pain would have to be faced.

At that time no voice—neither audible nor inaudible—tells me that instead and in spite of all the pain, I've just begun to face the most puzzling, intriguing, fascinating, questioning, demanding, yet exceptionally rewarding time of my life.

2

Memories

"Oh better than the minting
of a gold crowned king
Is the safe kept memory
Of a lovely thing."
—Sarah Teasdale

My evening walk with Hansi has become a task filled with mixed emotions. When Bob was alive, he and I had a routine: I would take Hansi for his morning walk, Bob would handle the evening excursion. Now I'm doing both.

The dog and I drag each other along—he, because he is already ten years old and has always had the hip-dysplasia problem so common to German shepherds, along with other ailments; I, because it's uphill, and I'm worn and weary from the emotional and physical strain connected with Bob's sudden and unexpected death.

In spite of all this I look forward to the evening walks, because then I hear Bob's voice as though he walks right next to me. Mostly we talk about personal matters, but he also tells me some interesting things, usually containing a word I don't know, which then forces me upon returning home to grab the dictionary. Treading the path that Bob took, I can get a sense of his presence, recapture a touch of that which was.

But I have doubts about the reality of my communication. Is the pain I feel over the loss of my beloved life partner so great that my mind is now searching for unreal answers as a defense mechanism? I doubt it. I've seen too much of the difficult side of life: war, hunger, terror, divorce, insecurity. Nevertheless, I'll continue.

Maybe, if I open my mind to something BEYOND the concepts commonly accepted as "reality," I shall eventually be more convinced.

Hansi and I gradually work our way uphill. I consciously absorb the caressing comfort of the balmy evening air, forgetting the past, just concentrating on the moment—this moment, step by step, alone.

Oh, Bob... *you* used to do that... there is the memory again.

Almost as though in answer to an unasked question, I suddenly hear Bob's voice again: "Go home, Inga, and read Ruth Montgomery's book *Companions Along the Way.* You'll find something in it that'll convince you."

Strangely enough I'm not shocked by hearing his voice again. Calmly I ask, "How will I know when I've come across it?"

"You'll know." He sounds quite sure.

I am amazed. The books by Ruth Montgomery have been a permanent reading project for Bob and me. I forgot who introduced us to her writings, but Bob and I found them fascinating and informative. She was a Washington reporter (certainly a profession requiring accuracy, an alert mind, and a sense of reality) who had been friendly with Arthur Ford, a so-called "medium" or "psychic." After he had died, she states she heard from him, with the suggestion to participate in "automatic writing." From this experience came several books, containing very interesting information related to matters of life after death, more than one life in a body, Jesus, other spiritual topics, Edgar Cayce, and so on. Bob had read all of her books and found them fascinating, but one book, *Companions Along the Way,* gave him reason to critique. "She really goes a bit too far in this one," he had said with a mixture of disappointment, mockery, and sarcasm. "What's the matter with her! I get the feeling she 'had a thing' for this Arthur Ford! It's Arthur Ford here, Arthur Ford there . . . I can accept most of the things she's written about, but this one is too 'way out' for my taste!" I hadn't read that book—Bob's dislike had influenced me; besides, there was too much to do and I had little time for reading.

The walk back home goes fast. That's really something: Bob tells me to read a book he had mocked and disparaged. Now he's telling me there's something in it that relates in some way to my experience. It would certainly prove one thing: that I didn't make up this communication. It wouldn't make any sense to fabricate something from a source about which I was uninformed.

I can't wait to start reading.

When I arrive at page 45, I stop. I know I've found what Bob was referring to!

My heart starts pounding as I read: "The initiation Jesus underwent at Brotherhood gatherings in Egypt, Persia, India, and elsewhere dealt with the understanding of universal laws as they pertain to physical matter, and the means of disassembling ions and atoms so that they can be reassembled on the other side of a wall or barrier. Understanding the law of harmony in music and color. How to heal and what to do about those who would not believe without seeing with their physical eyes . . . "

My God, "the law of harmony in music and color" is a *symphony!*

And as to "those who would not believe without seeing with their physical eyes"—that was I!

I am shaking slightly.

I had not touched or looked at the book. Coincidence? Perhaps. And yet . . .

Why of all the books in the house, why this one—the only one to have a passage in it pertaining to a symphony?

I go to bed, but I cannot sleep. My mind is racing.

I must do some serious thinking.

What *do* I believe? Is it wrong to believe in such a kind of communication? But if it *does* exist, why *not* believe it? Truth is certainly essential for reality. But is a truth that can't be proven really a truth? And why would a person rather believe in so-called "coincidence" than the possibility of finding one more reality?

It's a known fact that the full capacity of our brain is not yet fully utilized, only a small part of it. Why should occurrences of communication with another dimension of "being" not be possible, *if* such other dimensions exist? But *do* they exist? I have read enough about these matters that I'm aware of the controversy surrounding such subjects.

One thing is certain, though: I can be reasonably sure that I'm not losing my mind. My thinking is rational.

I fall asleep with a feeling of comfort and gratitude.

"Inga," says the voice on the phone, "I shall be in Baltimore the day after tomorrow. It will be so good to see you." It's Margaret, Bob's daughter from his previous marriage. Her voice leaves a subtle trail of pain behind. I can picture her: that beautiful face with her father's eyes; the pert little haircut; her brown hair; the graceful movements of her tiny, slender, lithe figure; her brilliant mind, always ready with understanding and compassion in any debate, yet presenting a logical and sensible viewpoint. "My little Philadelphia lawyer," Bob had always referred to her when we talked about our children. That subject had been another factor in bonding our relationship: we both experienced the pain of a failed marriage involving children.

She was already an adult when I first met her in person.

Her mother had taken the four children to Oregon when Bob and she divorced. Bob's anger and resentment at that act only showed occasionally—most of the time he didn't discuss it. But I could sense it and tried to counteract it by corresponding with his children, thus keeping him informed and to some degree involved.

We took care of each other's needs, Bob and I. We shared our joys and our pain, our fortunes and misfortunes. We nurtured and comforted each other, and we debated and argued, but always with love. Our children were an inseparable part of that love.

Margaret's visit is a vision of comfort that I cherish ... But shall I tell her about the communication with her father? Would she be concerned about my mental health, thinking that I was hallucinating? After all, she had received her doctorate in psychology some time ago. Her thinking is clear and precise. Perhaps, if I were to ask Bob tonight during the evening walk what to do, I would get an answer.

As I'm busy with the task of bringing the guest room in order for her, my mind again occupies itself with memories. That's all I've got left now, I think with a tinge of bitterness against fate. I quickly divert myself by picturing Margaret that evening during her last visit here with her husband George. It was a rare occasion that both of them could come, and Bob and I were delighted. We had bought tickets for a night out on our favorite pleasure boat, the "Lady Baltimore."

It had been one of those softly sensual summer evenings, the kind that makes you wonder whether you were really on earth or somewhere in a long lost world of wondrous fairy tales and myths.

Before the boat set off, we stood and looked over the harbor: lights in brilliant splendor choreographed new dance forms onto the water around the horizon's softly subdued twilight and the silhouettes of the surrounding buildings; the air was balmy and slightly breezy; and the music, though loud, was exciting and stimulating.

The "Lady Baltimore" moved sleekly along the water, toward the Bay.

Looking across at Bob, Margaret, and George, attempting to have a conversation despite the loud music, their faces relaxed and joyous, I felt a surge of happiness, of overwhelming fortune. My own two children were my blessing, but to have Bob's also in my life and have their love, too, was perhaps more than I deserved.

After dinner we went up on deck.

The night breeze caressed our cheeks, our hair, our skin, like the touch of a butterfly wing.

In the distance we saw the diminishing lights of the city. For a moment I thought back to 1958, the year I arrived in America: one of millions of immigrants, frightened but with hope for the future, leaving behind a way of life. How different my life had been until I met Bob.

I looked over to Bob, and my heart filled with an overwhelming love. Did he sense what was going on inside me? He didn't look at me, but suddenly I felt his hand in mine, gently squeezing.

"Oh, Inga," I heard Margaret's soft, clear voice beside me, "this is a magical evening . . . sheer magic." She put her arms around my waist, and we were both standing at the railing, absorbed in silent meditation, looking into a distance of dreams.

Yes," I said softly, "these are the times one cherishes: memory builders."

And now she was coming for a visit. How painful it must be for her to come and see the place of her childhood without the all-important factor of her father's presence to greet her.

Momentarily I can feel not just my own, but also her pain invading my soul again. Quickly I transport my thinking to tonight: I *shall* ask Bob—he'll have an answer for me! He'll tell me something that'll make Margaret feel good, make her believe that he's alive in another form.

As expected, Bob *does.*

Somehow it doesn't surprise me, although once again I have to fight off my all too rational thinking—it could be expected that I *would* want to fabricate something out of the desire to help Margaret deal with this visit. But I also know that Margaret probably feels the same way; she wants to help *me* cope.

Once again Hansi and I are trudging along Circle Road. The ground is still moist from a previous rainfall, and the air smells of mushrooms. I love that smell: rich, heavy, suggesting the fertility of earth, of life.

After I've placed my question to Bob, he says, "Just give her one word: 'violets.' She'll know."

He gives me another message, which I have to memorize since it is quite complex. It seems almost a professional or scientific one.

I hurry home so as to not forget what he told me and to write it down.

It no longer seems strange to me that on my evening walk with my dog I have a silent conversation with my dead husband. At this point it feels so comforting, so good, that I don't care one bit whether anyone else would believe it or not! Besides, I don't have to tell anyone, except perhaps my friends Doris, Frances, and Aline. They wouldn't doubt me, I know.

As a matter of fact, I can hardly wait to tell them of the latest message, because they already know about the communication and are not at all surprised by it.

Now, when Margaret comes, I shall be ready.

It will be interesting to see how she will react to all of this, especially the message.

Strangely enough, I have almost forgotten about the "violets"—I am concentrating fully on the other, complicated message, not realizing that that's a big mistake.

3

Visions and Violets

One more day, and then Margaret will be here and I can give her her father's messages. I wonder if they will make any sense to her. If they do, then I shall be more likely to believe that what I'm experiencing is genuine communication with Bob. I've found that there's a kind of cycle in my life. Every evening when I take my walk with Hansi and I hear Bob's voice talking to me, I am quite sure of the reality—but that lasts only through the morning of the next day. As the day progresses, I begin to doubt again. Then, during the next walk, when I hear his voice, I'm again convinced of the reality of the event.

Recently I had told Bob about these doubts. "I find it very

difficult to deal with an intangible, honey," I said. "Please tell me something that'll make it possible for me to accept what's happening."

After a few seconds he answered, "All right: picture a computer and a computer chip. The chip contains all the information, but this information is invisible to the human eye until it's placed in a casing and the electricity turned on. The chip can be transplanted from one casing to another; the information stays the same. You can also add on to this information. The casing is nothing without the chip and electricity—*they* are the vital factors. Compare that to the human body, soul, and life."

I thought that was a good comparison, and I was all right for a few days. Then the doubts started again.

Pondering over all this, I remember one more introduction to the esoteric part of life.

Bob was a member of an organization with Special Interest Groups, one of them dealing with the subject of reincarnation. We had decided to have one of their meetings at our house. We were interested in this topic, although I can't say we were "believers." During various get-togethers we had discussed the impressive history of Edgar Cayce—a truly gifted, giving man. If Bob and I were not yet quite convinced of the reality of such esoteric subjects, it was probably due to our own reluctance to admit to a belief not commonly accepted by the general population—yet no one could deny the authenticity of Edgar Cayce's extraordinary psychic and healing abilities, his unselfish, giving nature, his integrity. He was respected by all who met him. But it wasn't until many years later, after Bob's death, that I recognized the full extent of Edgar Cayce's unique personality. For now, though, we were content to debate and consider some of Cayce's finding and thoughts—one of those being the recognition that the soul may live more than one life.

We were a group of about eight people. Bob and I were anticipating some unusual occurrence, but doubtful whether any would come about. We had also been reading some of Ruth Montgomery's books and were not at all sure what to make of reincarnation, but there were reports by other well-respected people and numerous books had been written concerning this subject. As a result, Bob and I had become interested in finding out more about such things. Perhaps it's the mystery of the unknown that compels one to search for answers that one's brain is not yet prepared to provide. We read a lot—we gathered information.

My husband and I had discussed spiritual and religious matters at various times. The promise of "life everlasting" relayed in religious texts and in churches was a wonderful thing, but it was vague, difficult for me to visualize. My earlier childhood and teen-age experiences in life had taught me that blind faith could be dangerous—with the exception of belief in the existence of God and the Son of God. God was knowledge without visible proof, and in its highest form it was perfect and complete trust and love.

We had discussed the subject of more than one life in a body. Although I found the idea fascinating, I had trouble aligning it with my traditional religious values. Was it "heresy" to believe in such a concept? These issues could be debated hour after hour without proof of *anything*—whether right or wrong. As far as I could determine, the belief in reincarnation was not a *denial* of traditionally accepted religious concepts and teachings, but rather an *extension*. Perhaps it was all a matter of relativity or perception.

My friends Doris, Eric McKeever, and various others had introduced us to the writings of Edgar Cayce. We had had many discussions concerning this concept of life. Certainly we had found it extremely impressive, and most likely it was the foundation to further our thoughts related to the subject matter. In addition, it prompted us to start reading Ruth Montgomery's books. Bob read more than I did—he had more leisure time, and he would fill me in on what he had read.

Now Bob and I were facing the possibility of a small vision of things possible. Would it work?

After the group had arrived, we socialized for about an hour, getting to know each other's thoughts, beginning to feel comfortable with each other.

The plan was for half the group to try to achieve a state of semi-consciousness through a form of self-hypnosis, while listening to specially chosen, soft music played on a tape. They would then relay all that came to mind to the other half of the group who would try to put down in writing what was being said—all on a one-to-one basis.

Nora, an attractive brunette with softly shaded blue eyes and a determined yet relaxed attitude, turned on the music. The "meditators" had placed themselves in a comfortable position with respect to the various seating arrangements, and the "recorders" were sitting next to them, pencil and paper in hand.

I lay back on the couch, listening to the music. The lights had been turned off, several candles were burning. It was a warm and cozy atmosphere. The music reminded me of a mixture of a romantic étude, medieval chords, and modern compositions introducing an image of what may resemble the sounds of space.

I looked at Bob on the other side of the room. He, too, seemed quite relaxed.

At first I was trying to shut out of my mind all that could interfere with concentration: noises, thoughts, movements. I could feel my body grow soft, all the muscles seemed to relax. I tried to visualize God. Certainly, as it says in the Bible, we were created in His image, but it seems to mean in a spiritual more than a physical image. We were the offspring of the greatest, most loving, most intelligent, most creative power in the Universe: a dream in the mind—or whatever one may want to call it—of the force that is to us at this point in our evolution incomprehensible. We are a living dream, a vision of greatness, and a vision ONLY, being so far from the original intent of perfection. And yet we're *real*, have an existence, have life, have a body. Do I love this omnipotent being, the Creator of it all?—How can I not, if I love what He created?

My body felt weightless, my mind relieved, relaxed, engrossed in an inexplicable gentle warmth, huddling in it, yielding. For the first time in my life I had totally given up all desire to control my life, and for the first time in my life I not only sensed but knew that my destiny was not what I achieved in this lifetime, but how I felt and *what* I felt about eternity in connection with all life around me; I admitted to myself that I was an inextricable part of *all* life, all existence. It was a good feeling. It soothed my senses and, once again, while yielding to the power of creation and God, I also knew I was given the right to make choices.

All these thoughts had taken only a few seconds. But how could I be sure that if something would come into vision, it wasn't my imagination rather than a so-called "past-life memory"?

Ah, I was seeing something: a few people in a little village. Their attire wasn't of the current time period; it seemed more like the time of Mary Stuart, Queen of Scots. Then, it was gone. Pity. It had been pretty. Very pleasant.

Now there was a scene from Holland, because the girl I saw was wearing wooden shoes and one of those funny-looking hats. Long dress. She looked like Doris, my friend. Then that was gone, too.

These were all just flashes of scenes, no one said anything. I had seen movies of that kind, my conscious mind came through to tell me.

Oh, now it was getting interesting!

There was a mountain range stretching before me. These mountains were different from any I had seen: different shades of yellows, browns, and tans. There was a ravine below me, leading up to the mountains in front of me, at a distance. I myself was standing on a mountaintop, dressed in a long white dress, looking over to the other side. Why did I feel so sad? The sadness bothered me. There were some people walking on the other side. They were all dressed in dark clothes. From where I stood they looked like a row of upright beetles walking along a narrow, winding path from one side of the mountain range to the other.

God—what a long walk! They walked slowly, as though heavily burdened. I didn't want to see them! Seeing them made me so sad. But why? An overpowering wave of pain invaded my heart, my total being, as if the collective grief of these people walking had found a wavelength on which to travel right over time, engulfing me. Oh, my God, their sadness, their pain were unbearable! I wanted to get away from here, from the pain, from the scene. Take me away!

The tears running down my cheeks into my mouth tasted salty.

"Inga, Inga!" said the guide with concerned compassion. "Come on, you're awake! You're fine. You're no longer there."

I found myself slightly trembling. My God, what had that been? What had I seen? Did I fall asleep and have a nightmare?

I looked over the entire room. Bob was on the other side; he looked relaxed and comfortable. I heard him talking softly, but couldn't understand what he was saying. Well, no matter. Everything seemed all right. Everyone looked fine.

"Want to go on?" the guide asked.

"I don't know." I was afraid now.

She could sense it. "It's all right. These visions or memories do happen. Usually it means something, even if you don't know *what* it may mean at the time it happens. But a lot of times memories revived don't have quite such an impact."

"What could it mean? I'm a very happy person—there is no reason for me to feel such pain. Emotional pain, I mean."

"You were in another life," she said simply.

Baloney! It would be a cold day in hell before I would believe that! Well, might as well see what my imagination would produce next!

During the next few minutes another scene appeared: I was near water. The water glistened in extremely bright silver-blue splendor; it lay calm. I was on a beach, feeling the golden sand underneath me with a feeling of great calm and comfort. A white gown, with what felt like chiffon, flowed around me, and I was on my knees with my hands at my side, letting the warm sand glide through them. I looked up to the sky; millions of tiny, shimmering crystals came gliding down and fell into the water in a splendor of colors I had never seen before. I couldn't describe the colors; they were brilliant, overwhelming in their variety and beauty. Suddenly I heard myself say, "I think I've just died."

All this time the music on the tape in my living room had been playing—at my words the music stopped. The tape had ended.

Had this been planned, it couldn't have been more timely. But it *wasn't* planned.

Two weeks later there was an Alistair Cook special on TV. Bob and I watched it. The theme of the special was "Massada." As I watched the first scenes, all my senses became alert. Somehow the scenery looked familiar: mountain ranges in yellows, golds, and various shades of browns—and the silhouette of the mountain looked somehow familiar—yet I had never been to that part of the world. Suddenly I remembered: that was the mountain range I had seen in my past-life regression session a few weeks ago!

Bob and I were stunned. Ah well, I told myself, I probably had seen something like it on some previous television show.

Of course, a few years later I know differently. Then it all fell together, making a whole lot of sense.

The phone call from Margaret telling me of her visit interrupts my reflections into the past. She gives me the time and place of our meeting to bring her home. My heart is filled with joy as always when she's here.

4

This Thing with Feathers

I 've always been aware of the magic of work: work, when you're worried; work, when you're sad; work, when the world seems to come tumbling down. Work diverts, it forces you to concentrate, it uses all your energies in a positive manner. Bob and I had a life filled with work. But we found pleasure in all we did, because we did it together.

Together—no more.

Pain.

Why stop now? a maliciously sarcastic little voice taunts. No! That's not the idea, I correct it. Work is *not* a sentence— it's a blessing. Alone or together . . .

I must prepare the room for Margaret. In the process I

almost knock over one of the antique candlesticks inherited from Bob's parents. As I catch it at the last minute, the
touch and feel of the cool, purple glass with dainty hand-
painted flowers on it brings back memories.

Memories: curse or blessing?

That depends . . .

Bob's father had once brought me the poem found in the
Dead Sea Scrolls, "The Salutation of the Dawn":

"Yesterday is but a dream,
And tomorrow is only a vision;
But today, well lived,
Makes every yesterday
A dream of happiness,
And every tomorrow
A vision of hope;
Look well, therefore, to this day."

How intensely fitting for me to think about that now. I
remember a day when Bob and I had one of the rare days of
leisure. Bob had been engrossed in a book by Ruth Montgomery, and I had lit some candles in the "big room," listening to some of my favorite tapes of music. The sun was
setting in a splash of orange glory, and the light came
through the array of windows bringing to life, through the
shadow-and-light effect, some of the things normally overlooked as everyday items: the purple candlesticks; the iri-
descent blue vase with the head of three swans for a graceful
handle, which our son Ronnie had given us as a gift when
he was a teen-ager and which, later on in life—against my
protest—he claimed to be a travesty of good taste; silver
candlesticks from our daughter Gloria; a windchime of
birds making a tinkling sound in the light evening breeze,
telling me secret, magic stories of foreign countries, of adventure; the gold-colored music box from Papa, which he
had brought as a present for us when he came from Ger-

many to the United States and which played "Little Bear of Berlin," making me just a little homesick so that I never played it. All the collected gifts and small treasures of two lives joined together talking, urging, remembering, yet pointing to the future, combining past and present . . . just as they're doing now.

"I've got a really strange, but interesting book here," Bob had said. "It's all about reincarnation."

"What's reincarnation? I've never heard that word before."

"It's the theory of soul migration."

"Ah, yes, that I *have* heard before. But I don't know much about it."

"People who believe in reincarnation believe that the soul, which is eternal, must go through several lifetimes as a learning process to fulfill its purpose: to become purified and rejoin its origin, the loving presence of God."

"Oh, really?!" I was slightly sarcastic. "Don't you think that's a bit of nonsense?"

"Oh, I don't know. It would make good sense, though, you know."

"Bob! You can't be serious!"

"Well, I don't know . . . I've got to read a bit more. And then, I'm not sure, either, whether I would really believe it or not. Some people would do anything for a bit of attention. Still, Ruth Montgomery was a well-respected reporter with a great deal of integrity. I just don't think she would fabricate something just to get attention. Besides, you may not know this, but the belief in more than one life in a physical body is not at all new. It's been lingering in the minds and writings of almost every ancient civilization—including Christians."

"Come on, now, Bob!" I challenged him. "Then why isn't there any reference in the Bible?"

"Honey, there *is*," he said patiently. "If you read the Bible carefully, you'll come across quite a few references to more than one life. There was even more in the Bible concerning the subject, but it was taken out for reasons well known to those who did it."

I didn't say anything—simply because I was treading on unfamiliar territory. Bible study, as much as I hated to admit and felt embarrassed about it, had not been my forte in the past. Perhaps I should change that.

Bob sensed something of my discomfort. He was never one to increase that and so he just said, "Well, honey, read the book, and then you'll have even a little more to think about." He gave me a teasing little grin.

His knowledge about so many different subjects always amazed me. He knew history, geology, archaeology, ancient civilizations, art, Winston Churchill, the Civil War, any other war, politics, foreign countries—his knowledge was vast. I had seen him read books that it would have taken me six times as long to read, without having half his understanding of what had been read. I had looked at him closely, at his graying hair, at the lines in his face now a bit more pronounced than when we first met, at his eyes always radiating warmth and kindness, and even when he was angry at me they never lost that little sparkle of love . . .

I always marveled at how he could handle my sometimes rather impulsive and explosive temperament. He took me "as is" with good-natured acceptance. "Your eyes are like flashing ice when you're mad," he had said once or twice, grinning away my anger. Usually, after a confrontation of conflicting opinions, we'd end up laughing. His sense of humor was another one of his endearing qualities. His ability and accuracy in building and repairing anything; the gift to reason with fairness, intelligence, and kindness; his logic and analytical strength; all of these qualities had built in me a sense of security I had never known before. I knew I could always depend on him. He nurtured and protected me with patience and understanding, boosted my self-confidence, and supported all my dreams and aspirations. I wanted to go over to him and hug him.

Before I had a chance to do that he put down the book and said, "This really *is* interesting. You've got to read this, Inga. I think I'm going to get the other books by Ruth Montgomery."

"I will. But first, I want to read some of the Edgar Cayce books, Bob. Now *there's* someone who interests and intrigues me. This man had something *concrete* to offer—visible signs of his ability. At this point I know very little about him, but I intend to change that. If anyone would be able to convince me that there is more to life than meets the eye, it's he."

"Yes, I agree completely," Bob said, "he was a uniquely gifted man. I didn't know you had such an interest in him. I've already read a lot about him, so reading more about the subject written by other people will just give me more information to analyze. Anyway, right now I'm hungry. When's dinner?"

From that day to today time was like a racetrack, an obstacle course; a book not written, but lived; life in action, in motion. Absentmindedly, I pick up the gold-colored music box from Papa. I daren't open it to play the tune—Berlin, my hometown, is far away. And so is Papa. He is dead. Not much sense in reviving losses. But my mind, now on a certain track into the past, remembers . . .

Somehow, that evening, we never got to fully enjoy our dinner. As so often in Bob's and my life, emergency situations of minor or major proportions always seemed to disrupt our intent at comfort and leisure. That evening it started with the chipmunk and ended with Papa.

Bob and I had tried to bring a touch of the "peaceable kingdom" into our backyard. We fed all the wildlife within its border: ravens, small birds, big birds, chipmunks, squirrels, rabbits, raccoons, an occasional fox, and whatever else would find its way into the Chesney sanctuary. We learned a lot—not just about the wildlife, but also we were able to make comparisons with human behavior. Watching it all was educational.

That evening we heard the ravens making a big fuss outside; something unusual must be taking place. The ravens were the observers, the neighborhood protectors.

As I looked out of the window, I saw some movement in the small four-foot pool. A chipmunk had fallen into the water and must have tried for a long time—unobserved at first—to get out, but somehow couldn't quite make it. Now he was just floating without a struggle.

Bob and I raced outside. I picked the little creature up; it was cold and lifeless. I remembered the first aid course I had taken as a teen-ager. "Would you go and get a small towel, Bob?"

While Bob was getting the towel, I placed the little creature on a flat surface, pushing two of my fingers up and down its tiny chest, hoping to push the water out of its body. After a few strokes, success! Water, mixed with a whole lot of birdseed, came splurging out in successive gulps. Still the little creature lay lifeless and cold in my hand. I held it close to my mouth, blowing warm breath on it, then wrapped it in the small hand towel Bob had brought, where it lay for quite some time without movement. I kept repeating the procedure of blowing warm breath on it and rubbing its body gently with my warm hands. Finally, it moved slightly!

"Well," Bob said with a dry, but happy grin, "you did it again, Francisca of Assisi."

"Francis of Assisi was a bird man," I said, not exactly in good English.

Bob laughed, "Honey, that sounds like a novel about Alcatraz—you know, *The Birdman of Alcatraz.*"

I was busy trying to get the chipmunk to leave my hand. The little creature was afraid to leave the safety of solid ground and wouldn't budge. Finally I pushed it gently off onto the grass, where it took off like lightning. "Thank God," Bob said, "at least now I can have my dinner—cold as it may be by now."

"I can heat it up. But the ravens aren't going to have a dead chipmunk for supper."

I had planned to debate with Bob the issue of reincarnation and related subjects after dinner, but that attempt was thwarted by a phone call from my sister Chris, with whom both my parents were living. My father, who was sick with emphysema and who depended upon medication sent to him from Germany, had not had his medicine in two days. The effect was showing; he was miserable. It seemed that the medicine had been held up somewhere.

It was a thirty-minute ride by car to Chris and Buck's house. We found out that the medicine, prescribed by Papa's German physician and purchased and sent to us by a relative there, was held by the DEA in Washington, where, according to the letter from the agency, we could pick it up any time.

Bob and I assured my parents that we would go very early the next morning to do so. But first we had to get a letter from Papa's American physician. Papa looked gratefully at Bob. "I have such good sons-in-law," he said. My heart went out to Papa; he was so weak. He had always been a hard worker, a "doer," filled with energy and zest. Sometimes too much so—he could get rather "bossy" and would quite often get on our nerves. Now he lay there, a weak, helpless remnant of his former self, fighting for air, miserable. I was quite worried about him. Could not having had that medicine for a while be a threat to his life?

The next day turned out to be extremely strenuous for Bob and me. The doctor was only going to be in his office for a short time early in the morning; we were there as soon as he was available. Then we raced toward Washington, breaking the speed limit when it seemed relatively safe to do so. We were told in the letter from the DEA that we had to be there by a certain time, and we didn't quite know how to get there.

"I hate driving in Washington," Bob grumbled. "They always change the pattern; one moment it's a one-way street this way, the next minute it's just the opposite, and then one invariably gets lost. They're always building, building, building—are they *ever* going to get finished with that city? Light me a cigarette, honey, will you?"

"Have some coffee first," I handed him a cup of hot coffee taken from a thermos.

Finally we had made it. We explained the situation to the officials, praying that they would listen and not refuse to let us have Papa's medicine. I had made up my mind I wasn't going to leave without it—come hell or high heaven!

They explained to us that Papa could have his medicine sent to him from Germany, but it would have to be addressed to his physician, who would then give it to him. Gratefully and with a big sigh of relief we left and raced back to Baltimore, where we triumphantly gave the package to Papa.

On the way back home Bob and I were exhausted. We both took a nap. Before I fell asleep the fleeting thought entered my mind of how our planned discussion the previous evening about Edgar Cayce, reincarnation, and all the related topics had been waylaid once again. But I decided it had been a better thing we did: two rescues instead.

I have reflected on the past long enough. Time to get busy with fixing Margaret's room. It will be so good to have her here.

I wonder how she'll react to the fact that each evening I'm communicating with her dead father. Should I even tell her?

I'll let the moment decide.

After I've picked Margaret up and we're on our way home, we exchange information about the latest events in our lives, about future plans, about family members. But I have not touched the subject of the message. Perhaps I'm afraid

of not paying enough attention to traffic and my driving—
an intense conversation seems unwise at this point.

"Inga, at some time during my visit, could you take me
over to Macy's?" Margaret asks. "I want to get some of the
items they have on sale today. I have so little time to do these
things."

I'm only too happy to comply—Margaret's schedule is
hectic. We have a quick lunch at home and then leave for
Macy's. The parking lot is so crowded that I decide instead
of parking to drive around for a while and then meet Margaret at the entrance after a certain time period.

Before too long she returns, and we drive home. Now and
then I want to tell her about the message, but it never seems
to be the right time. Soon it's evening, and Bill, Bob's brother,
calls to invite us out to dinner.

The evening with Bill and Kathy is enjoyable and relax-
ing, and soon Margaret and I are on our way home again.
It's late, and we're sitting in the car in our driveway, taking a
few minutes to talk. The time has come; I tell her about the
message. Margaret doesn't say a word, but listens intently.

"Your father said, 'Tell her the concept is right, but the
psychology of it has to be adjusted to a smoother pattern'—
something like 'benevolent malfunction'—does that make
any sense to you?"

For a few moments she is silent, thinking. Then she
shakes her head. "Not at this point. But then, sometimes
messages like these can't always immediately be explained.
Someday I shall know what he meant."

We are both silent for a while, engrossed in thought.

"Well, it's time to take Hansi for his walk, Margaret. Do
you want to come with me?"

"I'd love to."

Almost as an afterthought I remember the "violets" message.

As she's listening, she turns white. "Oh, Inga," she says,
her voice heavy with emotion, "oh, God . . . " her voice trails

off to a whisper. I can see tears in her eyes. "Oh, Inga," she continues, "you can't know what this means to me..." I can sense how she is trying hard to hold back her tears.

I'm very much surprised at this unexpected reaction.

"You couldn't possibly know. When I came home from school as a child, I used to pick the violets growing along the roadside on Circle Road to bring them home to Daddy."

I can't say anything. It's not likely that even subconsciously I could have known that. Bob and I, when discussing our children, would talk about their schooling, behavior, grades, funny incidents, not-so-funny occurrences, and so on, but we certainly never talked about violets. I don't know what to say.

During the walk with Hansi we're both silent, walking along with our arms around each other. We're both trying to catch a sense of Bob's presence, but nothing comes through. Perhaps he knows that Margaret has something more to tell me.

"There's something else, Inga," she says as we're almost home again. "Today, at Macy's, I was looking at some eye make-up. I picked one up I liked, but I didn't buy it. 'Not now—later,' I told myself and put it back. But I looked for a name for that particular shade so that I would remember it. Do you know what it said? 'Wood violets.' "

We walk into the house, both of us slightly shaken up. Coincidence? Perhaps. Two coincidences on the same day? Possible, but not probable.

Naturally, there is a lot of discussion following this incident. At 3:00 in the morning we go to bed—tired, but happy.

Before I fall asleep, an array of thoughts races through my mind; I wonder if this may be the end of the communication with Bob. Maybe I had better start writing all this down—just in case there'll be more coming.

In a state of half-sleep the poetic part in me awakens the quick, fleeting memory of a poem by Emily Dickinson:

"Hope is this thing with feathers
That perches in the soul—
And sings the tune without the words—
And never stops—at all—."

Do I hope for more communication? Does it frighten me?
I don't know. In any case: What will be, will be.

5

Balance and Harmony

T he activity at the house is overwhelming. Somehow the noise of hammering, the ear-piercing sounds of sawing, men walking back and forth with boards, plywood, paneling, and various other materials, music playing (apparently to help make the work proceed more smoothly), and whistling—all add a sense of life to the usually so tranquil scene. The house is getting a facelift!

After Margaret has left, the home improvement project has started. Bob and I had planned it before he died, and I decided to continue with the execution of our plans. It involved a lot of leg work: choosing a company to do the work, selecting materials, making sure the finances would be all right, moving furniture and accessories from one room to another, making sure the work would proceed correctly, and so on.

Life seems to race, and yet time seems to stand still.

Sometimes I feel as though I'm living in a "twilight zone." By day I'm busy working at remarkable speed and with reasonable efficiency in a very normal, everyday manner, and at 11:00 at night during my walk with Hansi I have a conversation with my dead husband!

For the first time in my life I'm keeping a diary.

As the house is being torn apart and redone, my mind tries hard not to let memories dominate the presence of every day, but I permit myself the luxury of them—occasionally. My reasoning power is alert; I know I must not get caught up too much in what was—for fear of losing what is. Together with the love for all that was will sprout the pain of the loss.

Still, memories are powerful, and it's always unpredictable what incident will trigger their revival.

Today the "memory producer" is the refrigerator. It needs repair, and as I'm waiting for the work to be done, I'm remembering my first encounter with Bob's home.

After a few dates, Bob had asked me to come see his house. I was very excited; where and how he lived would show much of his personality. And it certainly did!

I remember the feeling of anticipation, as I entered the pleasant four-bedroom house, located in a beautiful, serene area of Baltimore. But then I was met with a shock. The whole house was almost completely empty.

There was a large room, fifteen by thirty feet, and by design and size quite impressive and lovely, especially since it was mostly all windows, but these were covered with brown bamboo-type curtains, and together with the brown cork-tile flooring, it had nothing to break the monotony. There were green-painted beams at the ceiling, the single touch of color to the large area. The only furniture in the whole large room was a brown maple dining table with four chairs. All this radiated a sense of brown gloom.

The living-room furniture consisted of one cocktail table and an old sofa with two arm chairs. The bedroom showed some built-ins and one single bed. The rest of the house was empty.

My God, I thought, living in that large house with all that emptiness must be depressing. But I knew all about that. What about my own apartment—without the children? Before there was a chance for the pain to well up like a fountain from within me, Bob said, "Come and tell me what you want for dinner." With that he led the way into the kitchen.

"She took the refrigerator—I could keep the freezer," he said. He opened the freezer door, and once again I was filled with shock. But this time it was dominated by laughter. The whole freezer was filled with ready-made, store-bought pot pies, neatly stacked, beef pies on the right side, chicken pies on the left. Dozens of them!

Bob saw the hidden laughter on my face.

"Can't resist a good bargain," he grinned.

After dinner we sat and talked for a while—on the steps of the "brown-gloom-room." He had put on a tape. "Love is wonderful the second time around . . . " the music intoned itself into our being, our togetherness. The soft warm light from the candles transformed the brown impression into an atmosphere of glowing softness, like invisible velvet.

We had talked about our children, our failed marriages, our hopes for the future, our feelings, our pain. Finally we felt the need for a change of pace and went outside. I had been curious to see what the outside looked like.

Huddled together in blankets, we let the cool fresh winter air into our nostrils.

Bob pointed to a little kidney-shaped pool. "We built that ourselves, too," he said with pride. "It's not deep, but enough to cool off in during the summer."

It was surrounded by an elevated, step-like brick wall, with a border of evergreen bushes; beyond that, old fir trees stood erect and proud. Their branches, covered with a layer of pure white snow, swayed slightly in the breeze. Crystalsilvery moonbeams, in uninhibited gaiety, danced around in this playful display of nature's splendor. Did they wave at me in a gesture of welcome?

"My world," Bob said softly.

I said nothing. But I knew that this man next to me in the blanket was beginning to mean more to me than I had wanted any man to mean—ever again. The disaster, heartache, and turmoil of a failed marriage was still too dominant within me. Still, here I was. And the stars, or something, were throwing some kind of magic down to me.

I could feel this haven of peace saturating me with its gift. I took a deep breath. For a moment all the bitter, painful memories of the past seemed to float away—disappeared like melting little snowflakes into the trees and shrubs around me. I wanted to stretch out my arms toward heaven, begging God to touch me—just for a moment, just a split second even, to have His immortal breath revive my questioning and tired faith.

Twenty-two years—and now? Has God fulfilled my request from that moment of long ago and finally touched me, let me know He exists? Did I doubt before? But why— why would He take away what I loved so much, change my life into waves of pain in order to get the message across? "One gets numb when too many shock waves hit the soul," Bob had said at the beginning of our relationship. I'm numb now—the light of my life is gone. Is my soul also numb? Can I separate me, the living physical being, from that undefinable, untraceable, unprovable, mysterious thing called "soul" that poets write about, people talk about? Does it even exist? Am I getting messages from an unknown dimension? And if I am, for what purpose?

All these questions—and Bob isn't here to help me find answers.

But perhaps, during my evening walk, I shall hear him again.

We must be a sorry sight, Hansi and I; two creatures dragging themselves uphill, each engrossed in his or her own tasks. I'm so glad Hansi is still around. He's more than ten years old; German shepherds don't usually reach a very ripe old age. I dread the day when he will leave me. But for now he's still around, sniffing at the roadside for whatever smells excite him, pulling on the leash to the point where I'd normally be irritated at him. But not now. My mind concentrates on contact.

And each evening, almost without fail, there *is* contact.

An image of Bob's physical person has never appeared before me, and I don't hear his voice out loud. It's just a voice in my head.

Tonight I've decided to ask him a question. I want him to explain more in detail what he meant when he gave me the word *symphonies.*

And once again, as so often since the beginning of contact, he does not go into detail. It is as though he gives me "leads," an incentive to further thinking, to further analysis of my own, searching for the final answers without his help. Most of the time, within a sentence, there'll be one word that I've never heard before, forcing me to go and look up its meaning. Is he trying to further my education? I asked him about that not too long ago, and he said (I could almost hear a loving chuckle), "Well, I've got to keep you out of depression—that's one way of doing it!" Am I projecting all of this—having known him so well, having been so close to him?

We usually start off our contact by exchanging general information. Tonight is no exception. Then, in answer to my question, he says, "Harmony is the balance of love—love of the Law of the Universe."

"Harmony"—that is connected to symphonies. But what is "the Law of the Universe"?

By now the walk has ended; we're home.

I race to the dictionary to look up . . . look up *what?* Well, perhaps I should start with *balance.* I've found that there are more meanings to words than one generally knows.

When I find the word *balance*, I'm in shock. There must be at least two dozen explanations for this word! It'll take me forever to find a correlation to symphonies and with it the meaning of the message! It's going to require a great deal of thought and analysis in order to come up with something that makes perfect sense. Once again I think I hear him chuckle, and I'm almost a bit mad at him. Leave it to him to make me really work for an answer!

Under *balance* in the dictionary I find:

"Instrument for weighing, typically a bar poised or swaying on a central support, etc.; power to decide as by a balance; state of equilibrium or equipoise, equal distribution of weight, amount, etc.; mental steadiness, habit of calm behavior, judgment, etc.; harmonious arrangement or adjustment, especially in the arts of design, something used to produce equilibrium; a counterpoise; act of balancing, comparison as to weight, amount, importance; etc." I shall not account for all explanations, some will be left out. It continues: "Dancing, a balancing movement . . . "

Momentarily I interrupt my study, because the flash of a memory is there, before my eyes: Mae, Bob's youngest daughter . . . New York . . . Bob and I watching her performance . . . happy times . . . Bob so proud of his daughter . . . then off to Bendahouse . . .

No. Will think about that later. Maybe when I've gone to bed. Back to balance: "A wheel which oscillates against the tension of a hairspring for regulating the beats of a watch or clock"—again I jump over some of the explanations—"to serve as a counterpoise to; counterbalance, offset; to bring to or hold in equilibrium, poise; to arrange, adjust, or proportion the parts of symmetrically; to be equal or proportionate to; etc.," and then: "to move in rhythm to and from."

Until now, when thinking of balance, I thought of weights, checkbooks, mental balance, or a tight-rope balancing act. Now, having read the complete explanation, I realize the profoundness of my findings.

It's so simple, and, of course, I've known it all along: the universe is based on balance. Or is it? Is it possible that there is a certain kind of harmony also in imbalance? Or balance in disharmony? I'm beginning to realize even more how little we do know—especially I. I'll have a lot of food for thought.

Will I get more information from Bob concerning all this?

Too tired to think any more, I go to bed. I toss and turn, though; the frustration of having information I'm not able to evaluate properly keeps me restless. Perhaps I should put it aside now and just wait.

I must divert my thoughts.

What did it say in the dictionary? "Dancing, a balancing movement." And there is Mae. Blithe spirit with red hair, exuberant enthusiasm in all her movements on the stage . . . youngest child of the man I love. After the performance, the first meeting with her father since she was a small child, growing up far away without ever seeing him. They were in each other's arms, hugging. I stood by, watching. She came toward me. "You must be Inga," her green eyes a searching beam of light directed right into my heart. And then she embraced me. I felt that slender little body with all the concentrated energy shaking a little. I held her as though she had emerged from my own body twenty-some years ago.

After the performance in New York was over, she came home with us. She had left it as a tiny toddler and had come home as full-grown adult. We got to know each other. The house was filled with life and laughter, with talks and running about. And now . . . ?

Now there's silence in the house.

Or is there? Am I imagining the sense of presence of all that was, like a photograph imprinted in the walls of the house, in its vacuum in which every action takes place, in the very air I breathe?

Imagination or not, it makes me feel good to think it's so.

And Bob still talks to me.

I'm not at all complaining.

6

Of Heart or Hope

"Yet I argue not
Against Heav'n's hand or will, nor bate one jot
Of heart or hope; but still bear up and steer
Right onward."

—John Milton

"I can't tell you how much I miss Bob," John says. "We always had such great conversations. He was so smart."

I don't quite know what to say. At this point I'm not sure how our foster-son would take it if I were to tell him about my conversations with Bob. No one would ever laugh at me, I know that—everybody has too much compassion for my loss. But without saying so they may think that I am projecting all this to make up for that loss.

From my chair in the living room I watch John pour himself a soft drink; the kitchen light throws a golden glow on his wavy, well-groomed hair, and his sturdy, well-built body moves with controlled speed. Coming back into the living room, he says, "I bought myself a guitar. I'm going to take guitar lessons." Then he turns on the television and continues, "I don't like it where I'm living. Could I move back home?"

Again I don't answer immediately—his remark (or request) surprises me. I hadn't expected that. Does he feel that I may need someone close by, now that Bob is gone? I know he likes his independence as much as I like mine; having someone other than Bob with me all the time is not exactly what I want. But then, maybe it's not such a bad idea. He could be of help with the heavy chores now and then. And I like his company.

As though he's read my mind, he continues, "I'd be gone most of the time—my job keeps me out till late, as you know." He is a chef in one of the nearby well-established restaurants.

"It'll be wonderful to have you here, John," I hurry to say. I wouldn't want him to think I don't *want* him with me. Perhaps he, too, needs to be close to where Bob's physical presence used to be. Anyway, the more I think about it, the more it seems like a good idea.

During the rest of the evening we discuss some of the books he's read. He's about the most well-read twenty-six year old I've ever come across. Small wonder—he has spent most of his growing-up years in hospitals, with much time on his hands, his curious, searching mind always on the lookout for a new challenge. Someday soon I'll have to tell him about my encounters with the unknown—*that'll* be a challenge for him!

Before he leaves, we agree that he'll move in as soon as the home improvements are finished. After he has left, I cannot avoid thinking back to the past and what brought him into Bob's and my life.

I had been working in one of the local, well-reputed mental hospitals for a few months, when I first met him. One morning he came into my office: long, wavy hair, a beard, jeans, and a disarming smile. "Guten Tag," he said in German with a light accent. "Sie sprechen deutsch?"

His smile broadened at seeing my surprised look. I smiled back at him and we started talking. I found out that his parents lived out of town, that he had some stepsiblings, a stepfather with whom he "didn't get along" ("the reason I'm here," he told me), that he felt smoking marijuana wasn't at all harmful, that he felt all these professionals didn't know what they were talking about, that the system "stunk," and that it was his birthday two days from now.

Well. That was quite a bundle in such a short time!

I found myself reacting with mixed emotions: with fascination, since he seemed very intelligent and well read; with anger at his misinformation; with compassion for his situation; and with the thought that perhaps, someday, he could be a well-adjusted and very interesting adult.

Of course, when his birthday came, Bob and I were at the hospital visiting him with presents, some German food, and some games, like chess. He won every game I played with him, and between Bob and him it was a tie.

"He's very smart," Bob said on the way home. "Darn shame he got involved in drugs."

Bob and I kept visiting him at the hospital whenever possible. "My God," Bob said one day after a visit, "he doesn't belong in a mental hospital. What has the kid done? He had a fight with his father! If they put every teen-ager who's had a fight with his or her father in a mental hospital, the world would have very few teen-agers walking around free." Then, as an afterthought, Bob said, the mischievous side of him coming forth again, "Yeah, that may not be so bad!" with a broad grin all over his face. "Think of all the peace that would give some poor parents!" We both laughed, but we also knew that John was a gentle, though momentarily rebellious soul.

"Putting him there was the easiest way out," I said. "But I wonder where he's going to go once the insurance coverage runs out."

"Don't get any ideas," Bob said, serious now. He knew me only too well. "We've got enough problems on our hands and have done our share rearing our children. The last thing I want or need is another teen-ager in the house with all the problems that entails. Visiting him is all right, but that's as far as it goes!"

Nevertheless, John did end up with us.

One day, shortly before the insurance ran out, his parents stopped by the hospital without seeing him, dropped off all his belongings (what few there were), and disappeared again, leaving no address.

John was not yet eighteen years old, and he had no high school diploma. Where could he go?

We fixed up the guest room for him, and he came to live with us under the provision "no drugs."

It turned out to be a very strenuous year. We had expected that.

The first thing we had to do—after the initial adjustment period—was to help John find a job. Boredom would be a negative influence; John had to have his own spending money, earned by himself, and he had to have the opportunity to contribute—even though in a small way—to the household expenses.

Soon that goal was achieved, but since he had neither car nor driver's license, it was left to me to take him to and from work daily. He wanted to save money for a backpack; he loved the outdoors and camping.

Some Sundays Bob and I would drive several miles to take him to a decent campground. We would probably have done other things without John being in the picture, but we always ended up enjoying the trip.

Quite often Bob, John, and I would get involved in provocative discussions at dinner time. John was an exalted, intense debater, and it was not easy for anyone to disprove or disagree with any misconception on his part, as his extensive literary experience made him quite knowledgeable in many areas.

It was not too easy to get adjusted to each other. As all teen-agers, John had his problems. Considering his background, they could have been worse, but he tried hard to deal with them. That was not always possible, and as a result Bob and I had many hours of worry and concern, and at times anger.

Occasionally, when he was alone with me, he would open up just a little bit to let me catch a glimpse of his pain.

Still, somehow I could sense a certain restlessness within him. I thought it was typical of all people in his age group; growing up is painful.

One morning, as we had one of our more involved conversations, I asked him if he was comfortable living with us.

"*Too comfortable,*" he answered. Then he immediately went on to another subject, and that diverted me. But the remark lingered within my mind and left me pondering.

Soon I was to know what that statement meant.

I was doing the laundry, and as usual I made sure all pockets were empty. There was something in John's shirt-pocket; it was a marijuana pipe.

In shock, I had to sit down for a moment.

He had broken his promise to us.

I tried to fight back the tears of disappointment. Why? Why had he gone back into the drug scene? Had we failed him in our effort to help? Was he unhappy? Was his addictive need stronger than our caring efforts?

That evening, after I picked him up from work, I confronted him with my findings.

"Well," he said defiantly, "I had planned to hitchhike to California to see my mother, anyway." He seemed rather casual about all this—*too* casual. I knew that he had found out some time ago that his family lived in California, but there was never any mail for him, and I hadn't expected that he would still be longing for his family. That was a very foolish notion on my part; blood *is* thicker than water.

And now it became clear to me what the marijuana pipe

incident meant; it was *meant* to be found! He had planned this! He knew that if he would break his promise to us, we would be *forced* to tell him to leave—that was the agreement.

The comment "too comfortable" now also made sense; the insecurities of his earlier years would not permit him to commit himself to any lasting relationship with anyone— at least not at that point. It was threatening to him.

It seemed he had everything well under control for his plan to hitchhike to California—from one end of the country to the other. I could not conceal at least one of my concerns: his physical safety; the other concern—that his mother, once he appeared at the doorstep, might not show any signs of joy—I kept to myself. I wanted to protect him from the immense pain this would cause him, but I also knew there was nothing I could do to stop it. I had to let him take a chance.

He left within two days.

Bob and I said good-by to him outside on the driveway. The morning sun was already awake, and the birds were singing with joyful enthusiasm. I tried to ignore the sadness within my heart.

Somehow a poem I had written some time ago while working in a psychiatrist's office came to my mind:

He walked into the room and stood before me
As if the wildest breeze had thrust him to the wall.
Alone, and frightened,
Like the trembling leaf, clinging
To the sustaining branches,
Yet apprehensive
of the inevitable fall.

His eyes: the wingless flutter
Of a captive bird, bent on
Escaping confinement . . .

Now ecstasy, and now despair,
Now loneliness, now torment.
Questions. Answers millennia away.
Resigning smile, lingering,
Left behind for those around to ponder:
Why me? Why me? It isn't fair . . .

A disappearing shadow, silhouetted
Against the sun, I watch him leave.
Go! Call him back! A gentle touch, a friendly nod:
He need not be
Alone
And frightened . . .

Instead my pen
Writes "schizophrenia" on his chart.
Next patient, please . . . But
From the distance, fading,
—Solemn intrusion to my heart—
A silent cry: please, give me back my soul, O God . . .
And in a dark, despairing, lonely moment
I curse my lot:
That though I have the desperate hope for healing:
Sometimes
I
Cannot.

We watched John walk down the road: bluejeans, sweat-shirt, backpack, hair nicely cut and good length, his muscu-lar legs walking at a speedy pace. He turned around once and waved to us. There was a big lump in my throat.

"One year of dedication within our life walking away from us," I whispered.

"From *here*," Bob said, hugging me, "but not from *us*. I have a feeling we shall see him again, mark my words." And then he added with a little laugh, "Yeah—and I'm not sure whether I *like* that or not! After all, it has cost us quite a bit of money—not to mention time and effort. It'll be nice to have fewer responsibilities once again. We deserve a rest."

I picked up on Bob's mood—it was better than crying. "*That's* the truth! And we could use a rest from all the turmoil in our life."

Somehow I had the feeling that Bob's hunch might come true, that we would see John again someday.

Under what circumstances was another question.

Memories.

They can invade the heart like daggers ready for the kill, or they gently move in and out like the flight of a beautiful butterfly.

I count my blessings that I have so many butterfly wings within my memory, my heart. My life with Bob let the daggers fade. There were so many—like the day my children disappeared. But I won't think about that now. Some other time. For now I'm concentrating on feeding my soul: my evening walk, talking with Bob. What will he tell me tonight? Maybe I should ask him to give me some message for Bobby, his son.

I met Bobby for the first time on the day of the funeral. After the ceremony three of Bob's children spent the night at the house—the pain of the event marring an otherwise joyous occasion.

I saw Bobby standing outside on the patio, looking up at the stars. He was not a stranger to me—none of Bob's children were. My husband and I had talked about them many times. From all I could tell, Bobby had inherited his curiosity, inventiveness, sense of creativity. But he grew up without a father. That was a painful thought, and seeing him standing there so alone on the patio, my heart went out to him.

I could sense what he was feeling: why now? why did it take so long for him to come here?

When I joined him outside on the patio, he kept looking at the tree in front of us, the big one-hundred-year-old pine tree.

"The treehouse is still there," he said. I could sense the hidden tears in his words.

"Of course." I hugged him. "It's almost falling apart, but your father and I couldn't bring ourselves to tear it down."

Then he said it out loud, "Oh, Inga, why? why now? It's too late," and he cried and clung to me.

"It's never too late, Bobby." What could I say? It wasn't his fault that he was living so far away. "You're here now. I do believe in life everlasting. I do believe that your father knows you're here." While I was saying this, I had to fight back the thought, "Why isn't Bob here in person to embrace his son?" and the pain that created within me.

The two of us stayed outside for a while, before we went back inside the house to join the others. All of us were close.

After the children had left, there was a void.

A void needs to be filled; I got busy with the task of surviving. They needed me; I was their living link to that which was.

On my walk, after I've told Bob what I wanted, he says, "Tell him to look at the road sign to the left of their house—it will give him some direction."

I ponder over that message—naturally. I'm not sure whether I should tell Bobby about that. Suppose I'm making all this up, and then Bobby is terribly disappointed? These things can cause harm. I enjoy my own messages—but when they involve other people I hesitate: too much responsibility.

Nevertheless, I will *have* to deliver the message. I have no right *not* to do so. I must believe in the reality of what's happening and, therefore, withholding information, especially if it could help, could prove to be a big mistake.

7

In a Dark Time

"In a dark time, the eye begins to see . . . "
—Theodore Roethke

I had been invited by Aline to lunch at Peerce's Planta-
tion. This is one of the most popular restaurants
within the Maryland area, the food is excellent, the ride to
Peerce's is filled with beautiful scenery, and it provides a
marvelous view of the Loch Raven reservoir.

Dear Aline, my friend, you couldn't have known that this
was the place Bob took me on our first date. Will being there
under the current circumstances be an emotional upheaval
with pain, or will it be soothing, healing?

On my way over there I reminisce to that first date. I wore
a black woolen lace dress, very simple in cut and style, with
a rhinestone question mark as the only adornment. Bob

49

had looked at me with open admiration—at first. Then he identified the jewelry as a question mark, pointed to it and said, with raised eyebrows and cheeky grin, "Hmmm—very interesting."

We had a delicious dinner. Going out to dinner was a luxury to me anyway, but to be at Peerce's with a good-looking and charming man—it was *ultimate* luxury!

We talked and talked and talked, getting to know each other. Finally, with some subtly disapproving looks from the waiter, we left. It was late, and the cold November night air hit our faces. Bob was trying to start the car: no response. He tried again. And again. The car was silent.

"O God, Inga," Bob said embarrassed, "I think I'm out of gasoline." This was the first time he received an inkling of my temper—I was furious. Fancy, trying that old trick of "running out of gas" on me! The nerve of him! I let him know how I felt in no uncertain terms! He looked at me in my wrath, not sure whether he should laugh or cry. Finally he had succeeded in calming me down. As though that was a signal for this inanimate object, the car, having done its little deed of mischief, it suddenly decided to start. "Thank God," Bob sounded genuinely relieved. "Thank God, it must have been that stupid starter again. I've had trouble with that lately." I didn't respond. I still wasn't quite convinced about his sincerity. But he did drop me off at my apartment, and we said good-night.

As Aline and I drive along toward Peerce's, these are warm, good memories. Out of the corner of my eye I catch some of the beautiful surroundings.

Old fir trees lining the road: staunch, serene, determined guardians of the Holy Grail. Their vision is nourishment for my depleted soul. Sunlight peeks through their branches, twinkling and dancing and teasing each other; will-o'-the-wisps in motion. The water of the reservoir sparkles from the brilliance of its source: *light*. Oh, for the light. I need light as much as all living things. But the light of my life is gone.

No! That's wrong! The light comes from another source; it comes from God. Bob and I shared that light. Now I should think he has this light in another place; it doesn't mean either one of us has lost it.

There is Peerce's—how do I feel?

Strangely enough I feel good. As a matter of fact, I feel better than I had dared hope. Why?

There is the dear, smiling face of Aline. Her smile is trying to cover up her sadness; she wants to comfort me, not confront me with her own sadness concerning Bob's absence. As always, she is stylishly dressed, with immaculate taste and well-chosen, good-quality jewelry.

We have a drink and order lunch. I can't believe how *good* I feel. I don't understand this. Am I blocking out the pain? Or is there something here that makes me feel that way, some unseen power or force or presence? Will it last? Or will it go away once I leave here? Oh, please, don't go away, feeling. I can survive this way. It won't be all that long, and then I'll be with my Bob again. If this feeling stays till then, I can make it. But it won't. My sense of reality tells me that it *can't*. But I'll enjoy it while it lasts, while I can.

Aline, in talking to me, is positive in everything she says. Her spiritual feelings are strong, her intellect is superb, the way she expresses herself is uniquely hers and hers alone. No doubt she does have an uplifting manner about her.

I feel a sense of loss after we've parted, but I'm on my way to see my sister Monika, where I'll pick up my mother who wants to stay with me for a while. By the time I've reached Monika's, the comfortable feeling is beginning to leave me. I had expected it.

I'm trying to block out the memory of the last day.

Bob's words, "Honey, I'll *always* be with you," are resounding in my heart.

My mother's presence is now something I see with mixed emotions. Something is wrong; she is very quiet, withdrawn. This could be blamed on the shock of Bob's death, but her right arm and leg are constantly moving in jerky, involuntary movements. I call her doctor to see if a tranquilizer might help. He prescribes some, and they seem to help, but then I find her sitting in her chair with her head laid back on the edge of the chair, eyes closed, her mouth open. Each time I see her like that, my heart skips a few beats: O God, no! Not she, too! The same happens when I take her with me for a ride in the car, and then I have to watch my driving so that I don't cause an accident.

Having her with me was supposed to be a help to me—it has turned out to be an emotional burden. But I can't tell her that; she always wants to help. I can't hurt her.

Finally my sister Chris and I decide to get her to the doctor for a thorough exam. The result is that Mom has had a minor stroke. Thank God the damage is not too bad.

I have been to the lawyer concerning the last will and finances.

The fact is that Bob had no pension coming, and I'm too young to receive Social Security. That means the only income is from some investments—and that's not quite enough to meet all expenses. Perhaps I could rent out two rooms.

Seeing Hansi trudge along beside me on my evening walk, I wonder how long it will be before he is taken away from me.

I ask Bob, "Do animals have intelligence, a soul?"

Bob remembers my love for animals and the interest in their behavior. Once we devised a test to see how much and what kind of a response we would get from our German shepherd. We came up with a response to a vocabulary of about eighty words—no intonations used. Watching the behavior of all the wildlife—domesticated included—around us, we learned a lot about survival.

"Yes," Bob says now, "in a very small way. They collect

their thoughts from the universal flow."

What?! I ask him to explain in more detail.

"No," he says casually, "you have to do your own thinking and analysis. Read and search and think."

Well! My work is cut out for me! But he knows what he's doing; use my mind to overcome grief and avoid depression.

"We have to connect our thoughts," he continues. "That's what keeps us connected—other than love."

I want to know something else. "You know, those so-called 'heavenly computers' that Ruth Montgomery mentions in her book—do they really exist?"

He answers neither yes nor no, but what comes shocks me into disbelief. He says, "The 'thought collection bins' are the Black Holes."

Am I losing my mind? I must be hallucinating.

For now, though, I put all of this aside and ask instead if this could also be the place where the "akashic records" are being kept. The akashic records are, according to statements by Cayce and others, each single thought of every individual preserved throughout eternity—just like information placed on a computer chip, accessible for those seeking this information at some time or other.

"No," he says, "that's an altogether different matter, but it's too much for one day. Some other time. But think about all I've told you so far."

Margaret calls from California. She says that her father had told her that he had phlebitis. What?! I can't believe it! It's impossible! I feel shock; has my life with Bob been a lie? I thought I knew everything about him. He could not possibly have hidden anything like this from me. We were much too close.

After discussion back and forth, she realizes that it *was* a mistake—it was someone else who had told her he had phlebitis. It relieves me; the doubts almost killed me. But it shows me what great shock can do to people.

Then Bill, Bob's brother, calls. He wants to know if I would be able to find the deed to the other grave site of my father-in-law's. There should be two; the second one intended for Helen, their aunt.

This is not a good day. Is there no trust that I can take care of things? Do people consider me only half a person now?

I feel nauseated. Lately I have been having stomach pains. Then I tell myself that no one wants to hurt me; *everyone* is in shock. But I can't wait for my evening walk with Hansi—Bob will make me feel better.

When he does tell me to forget the unpleasant, disturbing events of the day and not to take them too seriously, I accept that with gratitude but also—again—with doubts. Am I projecting all of this out of my need for his presence?

I try to rationalize *for* the reality of the communication. Bob, in his current life form, would remember the routine we had when he was still in a physical form. Since I am now doing what he had been doing when alive, he would know that any communication would have to take place at a time when I was totally alone and, therefore, open to receive—much like a radio station. The frequency has to be just right to avoid disturbance; and if you don't turn on the radio, you don't hear the music.

The next day Hilde calls. She's been my friend for a number of years. Now that I'm thinking more about souls and their development I appreciate her even more. She is a good soul. She, too, experienced the war in Germany, although not to the extent the Berliners did; she is from West Germany. There's quite a connecting thread between us.

I'm still suffering from all the emotional upheavals of yesterday. I'm weary and very tired. We talk for a while and then, out of my weariness, I say, "You know, Hilde, I think I'm not going to take my medication for a while. Then, maybe, I'll die, too. More slowly, perhaps, but it may do the job." I'm serious at that time and quite unaware at that moment of the lack of sanity in that statement.

Hilde is shocked. "No, Inga. *No!* You can't do that! It's wrong, and you know it."

I've never heard her quite that upset. She is usually very calm. "Look, Inga," she continues, now gentle again, "look. This, too, shall pass." She keeps on talking for a while, but I know I really don't want to live. Life is so burdensome. But after a while I think I have convinced her that I don't mean it.

A few hours later Gloria stops by. She hugs me tightly. "Mom," she says, and I can sense the hidden pain and tears in her voice, "Mom, don't let anything happen to you. Please."

I fix her a cup of coffee, and then she says, "You won't forget to take your medicine, will you?"

Oh, Hilde! She must have called Gloria and told her about the "medicine conversation."

But by now I have outgrown the depressed mood. After a while my daughter is convinced that I'm all right, and she leaves. I hate to see her leave. Everybody always leaves. For heaven's sake, they *have* to! I can't cling to people like a piece of gum!

With a slight sense of shame I recognize that the world is full of people who experience pain, and perhaps more so than I could possibly imagine.

Today is Saturday, and I'm consciously aware of the fact that I will never again see Bob's body sitting in his favorite chair, hear his voice out loud saying something, feel his hand in mine while he says "I love you." I must switch my thoughts.

My body needs nourishment, but I can't eat.

I call Agnes. She lost her husband years ago, and I remember seeing her in her grief. She knows how it feels, maybe she can help. After I've talked to her, I feel slightly better.

Then I call Doris. No answer.

I call Margaret in California, then Mae. No answer.

I am alone.

The words hit like a saw, zig-zagging their course through my body.

In the evening, though, there'll be a meeting to which Bob's friend Eric and his wife Florence are going to take me. I'm grateful that I've been included—so many times people are hesitant to include the partner of the deceased friend. I'm fortunate; Bob and I shared all our friends, too. The meeting will be one more link to Bob.

With some hesitation I tell the group about what I think was a communication with Bob, the "symphonies" episode. I need to hear how they feel about this, and if they think that perhaps I've lost my sanity.

But they listen intently.

Then one of them says, "Well, you know, Inga, there's that statement in the Bible that says 'there are many mansions in my Father's house.'"

I will have to think about that when I'm home again.

Eric says, "The philosopher Walter Russell was once asked to describe the universe in three words, and he answered, 'Rhythmic balanced interchange.'"

I'm stunned: that's a symphony!

Eric McKeever tells us also that he met Edgar Cayce's son, Hugh Lynn, personally. As far as Eric is concerned, it was Edgar Cayce, his philosophy, his gift of the "readings," his whole personality, that changed Eric's life forever—more than thirty years ago. At that time he was a doubter who turned into a believer.

What I've heard tonight provides me with a lot of food for thought. Good. It will divert me.

Another day is here. It's Sunday, and I decide to go to church. Though I need the support I'm hoping to find, I fear breaking down and crying. I don't want that. Apart from that, I'm feeling rather sick; my stomach is hurting.

After church I call my friend Doris. She is very loving and supportive, and suggests I read a book called *Initiation* by Elizabeth Haich. Although all this eases the pain of loss a little, the need for Bob's physical presence predominates. I want him *here, in person*, not just as a voice in my head!

Help for my depressed mood comes from a visit by my son Ron, his wife Dee, and little Kristin. They're trying hard to cheer me up. Hansi greets them with exuberance; Kristin hugs him. Momentarily I forget my pain. Hansi is so big and Kristin so small—she could use him for a horseride!

Ron suggests that we buy Chinese food for dinner. I volunteer to get it. On the way to the restaurant, pain overwhelms me again. *I don't want to live!* Who needs this agony? Why couldn't it have been me instead of Bob?

"Go on, Inga," says a tempting little voice. "Go on; all you have to do is direct the car against a tree—full speed! It's easy—then you won't feel all that pain any more."

"Oh, yeah!" counteracts another voice from somewhere, "and what if there is no immediate death, but a lingering disability, hah! What then? You want to inflict all that pain onto the children—yours and Bob's, right? Don't you think that losing you now also would be too much to handle for *them?* You coward, you! Who do you think you are that you can direct your own fate?! God?! Remember, there is a price to pay for such action."

At home again, I concentrate on my children and Hansi. I'm really not completely alone. Thank God.

Later, on my evening walk with Hansi, I have contact with Bob again. He is calming, assuring, loving. But I'm still inclined to think that I'm projecting all this communication. I mean, after all, why should I be so lucky as to have such fortune in my misfortune? Because, if it *were* real, it would mean that I would never have to worry about *anything*. I could just let things happen and rest assured that they would turn out well—and isn't that just a bit too much?

Still, doesn't it also mean that I would *really* have turned my life over into the hands of God? Isn't that what we are told in the Bible? God's covenant with us?

Perhaps someday, maybe even tomorrow, Bob will tell me something that'll *convince* me, without a doubt, that not only is there life after death, but a kind of life communication.

All right then, tomorrow come!

Come and convince me, if you can!

8

The Visit

"A friend is a person with whom I may be sincere. Before him, I may think aloud."   —Ralph Waldo Emerson

Something wonderful has happened!
I have company from Germany. My old school days' friend Gerti and her husband Heinz are here to spend three weeks with me. I am so excited! I haven't seen her in thirty years, and although the years show their toll, we discover during our first few conversations that we haven't changed, that we have more in common than we remembered. It's a glorious feeling—as though we both had climbed several mountains, separately exploring the world and the views, and then, having descended again, met and compared what we had encountered.

We're both amazed at how little the years have done to

separate us. Sitting out on the patio, we have ample time to exchange experiences and concepts. When I tell her about my new-found recognition of the possibility of living more than one life in a body and the conviction that death, as we conceived it so far, does not exist, she does not immediately answer, but looks pensively into the treetops.

After a while she throws me a quick glance. "I had an affliction not so long ago," she says in that quiet, deliberate manner of the schoolteacher she has been until her recent retirement, "and you know, Inga, that affliction was *my* best teacher. I learned how to meditate, how to see beyond the immediately visible, to look and search inside myself, to not judge, to accept what I can't change. I had to do a lot of thinking, and in the process I recognized that there really *are* more things beyond heaven and earth than we could possibly imagine. So your experience is just one more confirmation of that which I learned. And I'm grateful that we can be here to share these thoughts."

I place my hand in hers, and for a while we're sitting quietly, each pursuing our own thoughts. But we know we're talking the same language—and that even without words at times.

"You know, Gerti, what is so amazing is that during this first year of Bob's physical absence so many things which I must consider unusual were happening. Each of these events confirmed—or pointed to—a presence beyond my own consciously acknowledged beliefs, as though a kind, guiding hand were placing my pain into the clouds and softly eliminating it. Do you understand what I mean?"

"Perhaps," she says, throwing a curious ant off the table with her napkin, "perhaps not eliminating it, but absorbing it, transforming it into a positive force."

Now I *know* we're on the same wavelength!

"Some people would have killed that ant," I tease her.

"Tell me some of the events," she changes the subject with a smile.

"For Father's Day his youngest daughter Mae had bought him Shirley MacLaine's *Dancing in the Light*. You may not know this, because I'm not sure whether it was translated into German or not, but Shirley MacLaine is a firm believer in reincarnation and related esoteric concepts. The night he died, Bob was reading it. He died with it in his hands." Now I have to be careful not to let pain get the upper hand. "I'll get myself some more coffee. Do you want anything?" I change the subject.

Gerti shakes her head. "You mentioned his last birthday present, the phoenix bola tie. Can you tell me about that?"

And so, that day, Gerti gets the whole story: the violets message; the messages to Bobby, to Gloria; the violets on Peggy's birthday, the hypnosis and its startling results—the constantly appearing (and reassuring and comforting) "co-incidences."

"Then," I say, now very tired from all this intense talking, "I'm going to tell you one more event, and I'll shut up for a while."

We smile at each other.

"So, tell me," she encourages.

"I had not been looking forward to Bob's first birthday after his death, as you may well imagine. But you know what happened? A Shirley MacLaine special on TV—*Out on a Limb*—the one book that I could really relate to. Not so much her love affair with her English friend, but the second part, where she is spending some time in Peru. I tell you, it was made to order for me. The first part of the miniseries was shown the weekend before Bob's birthday, and the second part, the important one for me, exactly on his birthday. And you know what I did? I locked all the doors, turned the telephone answering machine on, lit some candles, and decided that I wasn't going to be disturbed by anything."

"Was it what you had expected?" Gerti asks.

"Oh, yes. Although I'm taking some of it with a grain of salt. There are some things in the so-called 'new age' genre that either I'm not ready for or I just don't fully understand or don't want to be involved in; I don't know. perhaps I keep myself too busy to get absorbed by this. Anyway, it was a wonderful message for me on Bob's birthday. I mean, it could have happened any other day or weekend, you know. But it didn't happen before—nor has it happened since. By itself, maybe not too profound; but *all* of these events in such a short time period put together are somewhat startling. I no longer believe in coincidence. Well, anyway, I better get dinner ready."

We have dinner out on the patio. Gerti and Heinz are visibly enjoying the tranquil beauty of the surroundings. A few squirrels and chipmunks watch us eat, hoping to catch a few leftovers. Now and then a courageous bird settles near us. The ravens are fussing loudly from a near distance—they always do when they're irritated over something or when they can sense danger in the neighborhood. A raccoon slides down from the tree nearby, attracted by the smell of food.

"Boy, Inga," Heinz says with open admiration, "you certainly have a piece of leftover paradise here."

"Well, Heinz," Gerti teases him, in an attempt at frivolity, "I'll get you a loin cloth, and then you can play Tarzan."

That evening we're making plans. They want to see more of the United States than just Maryland. They ask if I've ever been to Niagara Falls. I haven't, and so we plan to take a trip there and on the way back visit New York City.

At first I thought that they would want to go alone, but they insist that I come along—that they would pay the fare. When I protest, they insist vehemently, saying that they have been my guests for two weeks and they want to do something for *me*. As if their visit here *isn't* a gift to me, too! Finally I accept—with joy.

Strangely enough, during this time period the evening conversations with Bob have not been overwhelming, just a few words of contact. This makes me (again!) wonder if I haven't been projecting all the contact so far. Or am I too diverted by other things to tune in? If that is so, how easily *can* I be diverted? Of course, time has passed, and the conversations had already been less frequent before Gerti and Heinz arrived. Bob had told me from the beginning that it would not last forever. But I wonder if anything unusual will happen connected to Gerti and Heinz.

The trip to Niagara Falls is a magnificent experience. We have taken the train. Heinz felt it might be too much for me to drive all the way.

During the trip we have much time to talk.

"You know, Inga," Gerti says, "compared to your life ours is so dull. There are benefits to that, of course. A daily, though somewhat boring routine has its own benefits, but one has to watch that this routine does not become a stagnation factor." She hands me a package of crackers with peanut butter and cheese. "Here, I know you always need some snacks between meals. So I made sure you have some."

I am deeply touched by this. That's so typically Gerti, always making sure that others have their needs filled. And I hadn't thought of bringing some. Bob used to do that, too. Oh, Gerti . . . From within, though not physically, I hug her. And I really *did* need a snack—I can feel myself getting nauseated. That happens when I don't eat often enough.

Of course, she wants to know all the events of the last thirty years of my life. A tall order! We both laugh at the prospect of sitting around for months relating the unusual situations of Bob's and my life. But I do fill her in on some of the "extraordinary" occurrences—one of them the incident with John.

"How did it end?" she asks. "Did you ever hear from him again? Did he get to California? And what did his mother say?"

"Oh, he did come back after a year. He lived at a young friend's mother's house. The mother was divorced and needed some extra income, so she rented out some rooms.

John had a good, well-paying job, so financially he would have been all right had he not spent a lot of his money on alcohol and drugs. For a while there he was in quite a mess, but then he pulled himself up by his bootstraps and straightened out his life. He's fine now. Leads a very clean life. As to his California experience, he doesn't talk much about it. But he told me that his mother shut the door in his face."

"My God," Gerti says. I know what she's thinking. Then she says out loud what I've been thinking, "Small wonder he went into drugs and alcohol. No excuse, but certainly understandable."

I agree with her. "John is a very good person—he's not violent or mean. And he's wise and mature and perhaps compassionate enough to try to understand his mother's actions."

"That can't have been easy," Gerti says. "That does take quite a bit of compassionate maturity."

The subject now turns to our own children, and soon we've reached our destination.

We get a lovely hotel room, close to the Falls. On the morning of our first day there we explore. The first adventure occurs by taking the boat ride on the "Iron Maiden" close to the Falls.

We're standing huddled in our raincoats, observing the majestic and overwhelming power of nature. Somehow, in the human silence caused by the sound of nature's powerful fury, I feel myself removed from all that's worldly, and my heart is filled with a mixture of awe, love, longing, and admiration. "O Lord, my God, when I in awesome wonder consider all the worlds Thy hands have made; I see the stars, I hear the distant thunder: Thy power throughout the universe displayed . . . Then sings my soul, my Savior God to Thee, how great Thou art, how great Thou art." Have I been singing my favorite hymn? If I had been, no one would have heard it.

Gerti and I look at each other at the same moment. I don't know if the wet drops on her face are tears or water drops from the mist, the spray. I know that mine are both.

New York had been a very exciting, colorful experience, especially for my two friends. Now we're home again. Time races. I don't want them to leave. We have two more days at a condominium in Ocean City, generously offered to us by a good friend. The weather is beautiful, sunshine, warmth, ocean breezes, seagulls; the beach is hustling and bustling with swimmers and sunbathers in brightly colored attire. Then it's back to Baltimore.

Gerti has decided that this last Sunday of their stay she wants to come to church with me.

I am delighted.

As we sit down in the pew, Gerti looks around. Suddenly she nudges me. "Remind me to tell you something later on," she whispers. "Important."

I nod. The congregation starts singing the first hymn. And at that I'm once again overwhelmed with awe: Of all hymns that could have been chosen, it's a hymn I've never heard before—in *English*, that is. I didn't know until this day that the hymn that Gerti and I sang together in school at the age of ten existed also in the English language. It was a harvest hymn, showing gratitude to God for the abundance of growth and food.

Gerti and I look at each other. We both are thinking the same thing. In thirty years of my church visits this hymn had never been chosen before.

After church, on the way home, Gerti says, "You know that stained-glass window behind us in church? It had the verse from the Bible that was used at my mother's funeral."

We're both silent for a moment.

"Of course," she ponders, "it's a much used one, but still. And then the hymn, somehow I can't help feeling we're being talked to."

"People could say that one believes what one *wants* to believe, Gerti," I say, "and that may be true in my case, also. But who cares; it's much more comforting to believe it than not."

"Besides," Gerti adds, "you do have *some* proof—the messages and so on."

Gratefully I squeeze her hand. I wish she wouldn't have to leave.

At the airport the next day, as we say good-by, and as we're hugging each other, she says, "We'll see each other again—soon. This time it won't be thirty years."

We laugh at the prospect of the situation thirty years from now; we'd be walking mummies! The laughter eases the moment of good-by.

After having dropped my friends off at the airport, on my way home I reflect upon the visit. For some strange reason I'm not thinking in terms of three thousand miles *away,* but three thousand miles *ago.*

Are our human lives connected by an invisible network of tiny, silken but unbreakable threads, like a beautifully constructed spiderweb, and we run the course of each thread, meeting each other here and there, now and then, depending upon which path we take? Gerti, before she left, indicated some similar thought. She had given me a quote from a German author that said, "If only God would let us know His planned destination for us! Then we could much better tread the path we're walking blindly. But God does not give us roadmaps showing us ahead of time the difficult spots of our travels. There's always only enough light to see our next step, the one thereafter God will show us."

How profoundly visible that has been in my life.

Life gives us unexpected gifts. The gift of true friendship is priceless.

❀ *9*

Time, Ever-Rolling Stream

"Time does not become sacred to us until we have lived
it."   —John Burroughs

A few days ago I had sent flowers to Jeannie, Bobby's wife, for her birthday. For some time now I've had the feeling that things weren't all that well with their marriage, and it saddened me. I hoped that this would be temporary.

I was hoping that a phone call today would give me some better news—if not, then perhaps the message would help to set things straight.

Jeannie is delighted about her flowers. But she also says that the situation between her and Bobby isn't at all good, that she has been to see a lawyer.

I don't want to talk about these issues—that's between the two of them. Instead I plan to give her Bob's message for his son.

I have never been to Portland, Oregon, nor anywhere near there. When I ask her what the street signs are to the left of their house, she answers (slightly puzzled, of course), "One is called Irving, the other is called Peerless. We're living at a corner."

That tells me nothing. I don't mention anything about a message for Bobby, but we talk for a little while longer. During the course of that conversation, however, the subject of the streets comes up again, and suddenly she says, "Irving is a dead-end street, and it picks up again somewhere else."

Now it makes sense; that *is* the message!

I fear that there's possibly no chance for the relationship to survive. Of course, I don't voice that opinion. But I do tell Jeannie about my reason for my asking about the street signs. I'm not sure how she evaluates this.

After the phone call, I look up the word *peerless* in the dictionary: "Has no equal," it says. Of course! Bob has only one natural son—my son Ron is a stepson.

The next day I call Bobby, and this time I'm able to talk to him.

When I give him the message from his father, he seems pleased, but I have the feeling that the fact that his father has sent him a message is more important to him than the message itself. Perhaps he doesn't want to face its meaning.

After we've ended our telephone conversation, I am once again absorbed in deep thought.

The thought of divorce between Bobby and Jeannie disturbs me. But then again, Bobby's father and I, too, had faced these agonies. Is the love that binds two people together, for a while only, really love? Or is it fascination, unrecognizable as such at that time in youth? As for myself, I never regretted my decision to sever my relationship with my first husband. Perhaps I had fought too hard to make it work for too long to feel any pain over the breakup. When it was done, I felt relief, not pain. The pain had been there before, during the years of struggle.

And yet would anyone ever want to miss the glory, the exuberance of first love? I remember well the feeling of euphoria: someone—a good-looking, charming, wonderful man—loved me! We were married, had two children—a girl and a boy—traveled around with the British army for a while, then ended up in England, still connected to the service. It had been made difficult for us to get married because I was of German origin.

During the time of Egypt's struggle for independence to move away from British rule, my husband was sent there. The children and I were alone in London.

Those were difficult times.

I knew no one there. At that time I didn't speak the language well enough to get a job, and hiring a baby-sitter would have been too expensive. In addition to that, just a few years ago I was "the enemy"—the war had only just ended. Memories of that war were visible all over London. One could hardly blame the Londoners for not making overtures toward someone from the country that was responsible for that destruction.

I was lonely and very homesick. And the financial situation was that of poverty.

I needed to get back home—home to Berlin.

But how?

My husband had sent me the sum of ten pounds from Egypt—a small fortune for me at that time. It was not enough to pay for a flight for myself and two children, and traveling by train was risky, since I would have to go through Communist-occupied territory. If I could use the British military train, I could pay the fare and still be safe—but for that I would need a military visa.

Once my mind was made up to go back to Berlin until my husband would return from Egypt, it didn't take me long for action. I went to the War Office in London and by some sheer stroke of luck ended up speaking to the Director of Movements, or some similar title. He was a very nice, re-

fined gentleman, and he listened politely and compassion-
ately to my story.

A few days later I went back to the War Office to pick up
my visa and travel date—I was to go by ferry across the
Channel to meet the British military train to Berlin. The
gratitude I felt was overwhelming. "I'm going *home!* I'm going home!" was a tune exhilarating all my senses; I hugged
and kissed the children and danced with them around the
room. They didn't quite understand why their mommy was
so excited, but they happily picked up on the mood.

Oh, Berlin—to see you once again and walk the familiar
paths of memories.

How far away I was at that time from the spiritual recog-
nitions of the present. And how little I knew about the really
important focus of life. Yet all things have a meaning, a purpose, a reason for existence. Is it all about learning? Or ad-
justments? Or comparisons? Are we getting older in a motion
of climbing up a ladder, step by step—seeing sights along
the way that we couldn't see before, several steps down, because we were too close to the sight, giving us now a chance
to reflect upon what we had seen, what had been? And does
the number of steps differ from individual to individual?

Berlin . . . home.

There is an attraction to the place of our birth that is difficult to put aside, to forget. Berlin had held the extremes in
my life: from innocent, untroubled, carefree childhood
happiness to war, destruction, horror, and hunger; from the
exaltation and insecurities of first love to the pain of saying
good-by to and parting from all that was familiar. And now
there was the new greeting of "Hello, here I am again."

It touched me, with the war's destruction still visibly in
evidence, to see the almost frantic attempts at rebuilding,
as though getting rid of all the rubble would also remove
the memories of horror. But it looked good to me.

Occasionally a flash of memories invaded the superficial

layers of my being, entering—or trying to enter—the core. I saw us walking away from home; Opa, my grandfather, his "golden years" marred by the turmoils of disasters imposed by the actions of others and, as a final distress, the unknown whereabouts of his lifelong companion, Omi, my grandmother; dragging himself along with the phlebitis in his legs; Chris, only ten years old but so bravely facing this dangerous world without any audible complaint; Mama pushing the pram—its contents: the new bundle of life, Monika, my baby sister; and the most prized possession: baby food; and I, wandering amid the shells exploding around us, whether we would all come out of this humanmade inferno alive, and where we would spend the night. I remembered the pain in seeing all this destruction of life and beauty and tried to push aside the memory of the vision of Christ standing before me as large as the world saying, "Father, forgive them; for they know not what they do." (Luke 23:34)

Now war was over. Life had begun again. It was time to forget. God and Christ and faith . . . I knew they existed. So why bother thinking much about it? It was time to live, time to be happy!

And yet . . .

Someday. Someday in the future, I knew someday would come, where I would have to face deeper issues. But not now! Right now I wanted to enjoy the fact that I was alive, I was young; the whole world stood open before me!

What I didn't think about then was that before you can enter a locked house, you've got to have a key that opens it. When it starts raining and thundering and ice-cold winds and storms and hail surround you, and you want to find shelter within the safe, protective walls of a house, you need the key to enter.

Life has a way of teaching that.

All this reminiscing about the past has brought me quite closely into contact with the present. Naturally, when thinking about Bob's children, I think about my two. I'm worried about Gloria. She has taken Bob's death very hard. Bob was a good father to her, and his sudden and unexpected loss has left a deep void. If I could just convince her that there need not be that void, that sense of loss—after all, I still have Bob's most important element well and alive within and around me, even though his body is missing.

But how to relay that to her in a convincing way? I don't want to force my own beliefs on anyone else, but why not share a knowledge that is comforting, healing?

That evening on my walk I tell Bob about this and ask for his help.

"It's going to be difficult," he says. "She is a nonbeliever (or *claims* to be)," he chuckles, "and anything I tell you to pass on to her may be misconstrued by her as an attempt on your part to make her feel better. It would have to be something only she knows, and that'll take some time for me to figure out."

On the way home I'm trying not to think about some of the less pleasant aspects of "life before Bob," but somehow today diversion won't come. My daughter's pain has brought to life much of my own pain within me—but this time, just as a memory. I can't help but make the comparison between the past and the present. Before I knew Bob, life was an existence of moment to moment—to be coped with as well as possible, sometimes for better, sometimes for worse. When Bob entered into my life, I was living in a steady, stable flow of happiness and contentment, in spite of the normal disturbances of life situations.

Now Gloria needs help. She hasn't asked for it, but I know she does. Will Bob be able to come up with something that'll convince her that there are "more things between heaven and earth . . . "?

I'm sure he will.

So far, he's come forth each time.

10

The Phoenix Bola Tie

I have had to wonder why the communication with Bob concerning people other than myself only extended to some. Meda, his oldest child, had been living in Hawaii for a number of years; she had received her doctorate in sociology and had a great job. She had been married for a number of years and seemed quite happy. Bob and I had less contact with her than with the other children. But despite that, I felt a great deal of affection for her: being the oldest is not always so great. Hawaii is so far away, and I think Bob always suspected that visits would be out of the question and tried to stay aloof. Many times he started writing a letter, then never finished it. Somehow I always had the feeling that he didn't believe in long-distance love—perhaps because he knew he would never be able to put his feelings into the right words.

Since I had to do all the corresponding and since life was always a race for time, Meda and I had little contact, but I thought about her often. One thing became clear: Bob's children were hard workers and achievers.

It was difficult to tell how Meda took Bob's death, but during a phone call we felt close to each other, even though that was just a few moments.

Since there seemed to be no need for messages from Bob, there weren't any. Bob only responded to my requests—he never initiated the contact for others.

Today is Thursday, and I've just given Gloria the message Bob had given last night—three days after I'd asked him. "Tell her," Bob had said, "that when she baby-sat for Mr. Marsilio, she read a book. There's a message for her in that book. And also tell her that bumping into Mr. Marsilio was no coincidence."

The message surprised me, although it shouldn't have; time is nothing in eternity. Mr. Marsilio was Gloria's vice principal in high school. Gloria graduated about twenty years ago! When I first received the message, I had a hard time trying to figure out who Mr. Marsilio was and had it not been for Gloria's baby-sitting his children, I probably would not have remembered his name—at least not offhand.

After I've given her the message (by telephone), Gloria is silent for a moment. Then she says, "I remember reading *The Red Badge of Courage*. I shall go to the library and get it and read it again."

It's hard for me to tell how she has taken all this; she seems pensive. But one thing surprises me very much; I would never have considered her reading a book like *The Red Badge of Courage* instead of watching television while she was baby-sitting! With a slight feeling of shame I admit to myself that perhaps I didn't know my daughter as well as

I should have. Of course, when she came home from baby-sitting, she was tired and wanted to go to bed right away, so there was no chance to talk; and the next day would generally be a weekend day with sleeping-in. By the time she'd get up, Bob and I would be busy, and then in the evening she'd be with friends or perhaps out on a date or the movies. She never said, "Oh, I read this book, and it was interesting," a fact that now, so many years later, has impact on me. I regret I didn't pursue conversations more emphatically.

It will be interesting to see what will come from this. And what about the message about "bumping into Mr. Marsilio"? When I talked to Gloria, she didn't mention a word about having "bumped into" Mr. Marsilio. After not having seen or heard from her former school vice principal for two decades, it certainly would have left an impression had that taken place.

At least Gloria seemed not inclined to ridicule—either overt or covert. Not too long ago, when I had started mentioning the events of communication with Bob to some of my family members, I realized that for occurrences of that kind, one will have to be prepared for various reactions: either compassionate doubt; or a hint of an understanding and a sympathetic smile ("poor thing—she's trying so hard not to show her grief"); or a polite, but very questioning silence and occasional comment ("Oh, really?"); or—miracle of miracles!—a genuine interest combined with sincere curiosity and questions. Luckily, and very much to my surprise, I found mostly curious interest—and not only that, but after listening to my telling the events, I usually heard some stories of similar occurrences, convincing me even more of the reality of my experience.

The home improvement crew had arrived earlier and is now hammering away, making a great deal of noise. I'm glad I had one of the bedrooms located toward the back of the house available as a retreat away from the commotion. When John told me he wanted to move back home, it was with the understanding that this would take place after the home improvement was done. So now I have a nice large room available to me as a sitting/bedroom. Though most of the decorative pieces were put away temporarily, I had to have some items that were at this particular time very important for me to see or touch every day.

There are some photographs, a statue of Nefertiti that Bob himself had made from an existing copy from the Berlin Museum of Art, books, and some other knickknacks for some reason or other not put away. Then there is a wall decoration opposite from my bed so that I can look at it every time I want to: a small plaque with a poem Gloria had given me just before Bob died; it hangs on the wall on the same nail as a large silver bola tie, handmade by Indians, with inlaid turquoise, mother-of-pearl, and coral. It is the head of the phoenix—the ancient symbol of reincarnation, of life rising from the ashes. Bob, who in the twenty-two years of our marriage had never expressed a wish for any particular present or gift, had told me a year before he died that he would like to have a bola tie, and he described what he wanted. That puzzled me, but there was no reason to be concerned. Bob seemed in perfect health.

Naturally I tried to fulfill his wish, which proved to be a difficult task. Bob had made it clear that there were lots of bola ties with eagles' heads and the wings in a certain position, but he wanted to be sure that it had the wings *upward*. (The word "phoenix" was not mentioned at that time—that came later.) I knew what he meant; in previous years we had occasionally come across some of those Bob described. This year, though, they seemed to have disappeared from the face of the earth! I must have called every local and nearby out-of-town store; no luck. There were a number of them available, but none with the upward wings. I went to out-of-town places to look at some that over the phone had been described to me and were a possibility, to no avail. Finally, I seemed to be in luck. A local jeweler, who traveled and had connections to Indians in Arizona, told me he knew exactly what I wanted, and yes, he could get me one. They weren't cheap. I assured him that that would not be a problem since the children and I were pitching in together, but that I needed to have it in my possession in time for my husband's birthday. He promised to do what he could.

When Bob's birthday came, his present was ready.

The children and I were very excited. Would it be just as he had wanted? Little did any of us know at that time that this would be their dad's last birthday present.

Of course, Bob loved it. He had never been one to ask for anything—the joy on his face when he saw the phoenix bola tie was a gift to us.

I am pondering over these memories as I'm lying on my bed for a quick afternoon nap, looking at the bola tie hanging right over the plaque that Gloria had given me. Do I really have proof that life goes on in some other form after what we call "death" has occurred? And what kind of proof *could* there be? In church I hear myself saying, "I believe in the resurrection of the body." I always think of that in connection with Jesus, not myself or anyone else. I know I should, though. But then, what is considered "a body"? Isn't a tiny microbe, a seed, an atom, etc., also a body?

I had no idea that the incident of Bob's death and my communication with him after that would pose such soul-searching questions. And somehow I sense that that's just the tip of the iceberg.

From my bed I see the shape of the phoenix: intricate, inlaid, beautiful mosaic work, detailed to perfection. The wings reaching up into the heavens, like the wings of an angel. It's hanging from the nail over Gloria's poem, as though it were ready to take off in flight.

I get up to take a look at the poem. I want to read the loving words once again, as though their meaning would nourish my soul.

The bola tie is looped around the nail, with the phoenix

covering the first verse of the poem. As I'm approaching both, I see the phoenix slowly sliding downward, slowly, slowly, until it stops right over the poem's middle verse. Startled and curious, I slide the phoenix up to the top to see if it will slide down again and where it will stop.

Again it slides down to the middle verse.

As I'm reading the words, I get chills. But they are chills of happiness. It reads:

" ... just let it now suffice to say
That deep inside I know
My love for you is something
That I never will outgrow ... "

None of the other verses would fit, if this is meant to be a message from Bob to me.

For a few moments I'm too startled to move. Then my thoughts start racing. If the phoenix wanted to slide down— why didn't it slide down all the way, why did it stop in the middle of the poem? And why hadn't it done it before, or did it all the time? I have to be sure; I slide the bird back up to its original position on top, hang it back up on the nail, and wait. Within a few seconds it does it again! Again it slowly slides down and stops right above the middle verse.

I lie down on my bed. The tears running down my face are born of gratitude, wonder, and amazement.

I have to admit (with a slight sense of shame at my doubting attitude) that I tried to repeat this incident a day later by looking at the bola tie in the hope that it would do it again, even touching it a little to see if it would slide down—it did! But it slid down all the way, and no matter how hard I tried a repeat performance, it never did the same thing again.

It seems that life, or Bob, or angels—or God even—wants to be kind to me, convince me of things existing beyond our realm of current knowledge.

Gloria just called me.

"Are you watching TV?" her voice is just a little shaky.

"No."

"Well," she says, still with that little touch of uncertain wonderment, "I just turned on my public television channel—and guess what's on?"

"Oh, boy," is all I can say at that moment. "Oh, boy, *The Red Badge of Courage*, right?"

"Right."

We're both silent for a few moments. Then she says, "I can't say I believe, Mom—but I'm surely a little shaken up. I swear to you, I didn't look at the *TV Guide* before I turned it on."

"You don't have to convince *me*," I say. "I *know*."

Then I tell her about the phoenix bola tie.

She listens intently, without saying much. We don't mention the other message about "bumping into." That is, until the following day.

The phone rings, and it's Gloria again.

"This time, Mom," she says, "I *am* shaken up. Thoroughly! Here's what happened: I was going to Bell's" (a local gift store) "with Erika" (her youngest daughter) "to buy something, and in a last-minute change of plans we decided to go to Caldor's instead. And guess whom I 'bumped into'?"

"Mr. Marsilio," I say. Naturally!

"Right." Again, as the day before, we both are silent for a few moments. I want to ask her, "Do you believe *now*?" but I refrain from doing it. I *know* she does, but she may never admit it. What is interesting, though—and something she hasn't even thought about—is that Bob had said "her bumping into Mr. Marsilio *was* no coincidence," as though it had already happened! Which will prompt me to think about the subject of "time" in space and eternity. For now I leave that subject alone, though. I want to enjoy the moment.

Some time later, at a very critical moment in her life, Gloria will have even more reason to believe—but for now we don't know that.

I send a silent "thank you" to Bob—my expressed gratitude will have to wait until my evening walk. Who knows what he'll come up with next!

11

A Glimpse of the Dark Side

D oris, Aline, Frances, and Hilde are my friends and confidantes. To them I reveal my thoughts, the occurrences of communication with other dimensions (which certainly has Bob as its main source at the moment), and we have long and extensive discussions concerning these matters. I never have to worry about what to say or how to say it—they and I are on the same "wavelength." It feels good to be loved and understood.

I met Doris some years ago while we were both working at a mental hospital. It was there, and because of Doris, that the first contact with those things invisible, which I had put to sleep since childhood, was reawakened within me. She had read my book *A Time of Rape*, which told the story of my family and me within the turmoil and chaos of war and conquest by foreign troops, and it revealed to Doris more about me and my inner thoughts than I myself had intended or recognized. "You know, Inga," she had said, "that part in your book where you talk about 'Jesus standing before you as large as the world.' That part is my favorite, although I like the whole book very much. You're very high," she said with a sweet and gentle smile. I liked the way her soft brown eyes smiled even more than her mouth did, but I didn't know what she meant by "high." When you work in a mental hospital, "high" could mean "under the influence" of something! But that was then. Now I know what she meant.

That day after work, on my way home, I remembered the excitement and exaltation of the trip to New York with Bob; my manuscript had been accepted, we were going to the publisher's, and soon I would see my name in print on a book! It was like a fairy tale come true. Apart from that I was looking forward to experiencing—once again, after many years away from Berlin—the flavor of the metropolis.

Oh, New York City . . .

You, with that divided personality: half-decadence, half-refreshing newness; half-life, half-death; half-hope, half-desperation; but always, always pulsating and vibrating with the voices of the past and the future. You are a temptress. You are a hussy. You are a Grand Dame. You're half-sinner, half-saint. You pick up and throw away. You promise and then laugh. You tempt and then withdraw the golden glove. You lift up and then throw down. You are everything to some, nothing to some, and something of something to most. You are ugly and beautiful at the same time. You educate and you suppress. And you hide your miserables among the glitter and the glitz of the world, displayed in almost vulgar elegance—like an exhibitionist displaying your wares and your fables and your hopes and your dreams and your sophistication—and yet: you *inspire*. How do you do it? You attract the intellectual, the artist, the dreamer, the entrepreneur, and you say: "Okay, Buddy, sink or swim," and if he or she fails, you turn your back and walk toward the next one. You are the epitome of contrast. And you are either hated or loved—but no one can ignore you.

Bob and I signed the contract, went to lunch with the vice president of the company, and left for home—exhilarated, tired, happy. When, some months later, I held the book in my hands for the first time, my gratitude for my wonderful life and for Bob, who had encouraged me, supported me, helped with editing, and so on, and who had been my most fervent fan, knew no end.

Years later Doris, with whom I had kept up contact after leaving my job because of a temporary health problem, had been present at the Special Interest Group meeting, where I had the strange experience of seeing the group of people walking on a mountain range before me.

Today, however, it's Aline and Frances who are going to be my helpers. They are going to accompany me to a hypnotherapist. I have decided that perhaps the only way for me to quit smoking is going to be through hypnosis. But the first session is only for the purpose of seeing if I *can* be hypnotized.

The man who was recommended to me is a reputable hypnotherapist, Carl Schlotterbeck. The moment I set eyes on him I feel comfortable; he has a quiet, composed, gentle manner and, although he's not tall, his voice is resonantly powerful, yet very soothing.

Aline and Frances sit quietly in the background, observing. After about thirty minutes, I'm aware of being under hypnosis. It's a strange feeling; I know my hand is moving, as Carl's voice suggested, but I'm also aware that I'm not willing this myself. It amazes me that I *can* be aware and still have my muscles and/or nerves move, as it seems, on their own. Am I fully hypnotized? Carl had initially told me that I would be aware and not be completely asleep. It's a very strange feeling.

When it's over, Frances and Aline accompany me home, none of us having any hint at the surprising events that would take place at the next session. We discuss the context of this session to some degree, but I'm not really very interested—perhaps because at this point I'm still not too convinced of the reality of "past-life regression."

It's 10:00 in the morning—the phone ringing disrupts my letter-writing to family in Germany. Slightly annoyed I pick up the phone. It's Helen, Bob's aunt, who lives in Florida.

"Inga," she says, the tone of her voice displaying a haunting, disquieting urgency, "Inga, you *must* come here. You've got to get me out of here! I can't *stand* it any more!" Despite some concern I almost have to smile; the old stage training always shows through! Helen, in her younger years, was a very talented singer and dancer, who performed in New York as well as other parts of the country, and the years of performances on stage have remained with her; she reminds me very much of "Auntie Mame." She has a way of making something sound extremely important, even though it may not be, by the mere emphasis placed on words.

"Why? What's wrong, Helen?"

"Oh, Gaaawd, Inga," she says dramatically, "Oh, Gaaawd—you don't know what's going on around here!"

She tells me that she gets awakened at night by noises around the house. That the area is no longer safe. That she's had someone come in to place a big heavy bar in front of her bedroom door because sometimes it seems as though someone is in the house. That she's had hardly any sleep in weeks. That the house should be sold, but that she alone just can't do it. And would I come and help her do it.

I listen to all this with mixed emotions. I love Helen—she

was Bob's favorite relative. The younger sister of his mother. And he remembered her stage career and was always so proud of having such a beautiful, talented, young aunt. But to go to Florida? Selling a house could take months!

I try to calm her down and reassure her that with all she had done it seemed unlikely anyone would be able to harm her. And to pray for protection to the angels.

"I do, every night," she says emphatically.

"And when you're frightened, just call me—day or night," I tell her. She seems to feel better, as we end the conversation.

After the phone call, I reminisce about a recent, rather strange experience during my evening walk. It was an icy cold evening. Hansi and I eased and inched our way back home, and I had to be careful not to slide and fall on the icy road. My conversation with Bob had been a joy to my soul, but nothing spectacular had been discussed. Suddenly, at the end of my walk, I noticed a smell of flowers. Startled, I stopped—jasmine! The last time I had smelled the fragrance of jasmine had been in Berlin, during the war. But tonight, on a very isolated country road, in the middle of winter, where could such a fragrance come from? Hansi had stopped, too, as though he could sense something was unusual. I looked around me to see if someone could be nearby with perfume, but not a soul in sight. Besides, Hansi would have barked. He was very alert. Suddenly I heard a voice—it was not Bob's! After my initial shock had subsided (it had only taken seconds), I heard a gruff, female voice say, "Tell my sister to quit the booze, or else she'll be dead in two years!"

"Granny Mae?" I asked in shock, and then was shocked again by the recognition that I had called Bob's mother "Granny Mae"—to my knowledge only Margaret had addressed her like that. But I had the distinct feeling that I had heard the voice of Bob's mother, who died a few years before I met Bob. He had talked a lot about his mother, and I always had the impression that she was a soft-spoken, very kind and gentle woman. Many times I had taken a photograph of Bob's mother into my hands and studied the lovely face of the woman who had reared, loved, and nurtured the man I loved so much.

Now here was this harsh voice using rather rugged language—could it be that there were some other forces at work? When reading about such subjects, I was made aware that not all forces from the "other side" were *good* forces.

Carefully making our way on the dangerously icy, uneven road toward home, Hansi and I were glad when we were inside the warm, safe house again. And I remember with a feeling of uncomfortable puzzlement how Hansi had stood so motionless, without his usual attempt at going along *his* path instead of mine.

How very disturbing! And what was I supposed to do with *this* information? I had to do some very careful analyzing.

If the voice was that of some negative force trying to play a trick on me, imitating Bob's mother, then it was best to ignore all of it. But I doubted that. Why not find something more intriguing with which to upset and puzzle me?

So, assuming that I really heard Bob's mother giving me a rather profound message for Helen, should I tell her?

Oh, what a quandary!

It was clear from the message that Helen was considered an alcoholic—that kind of language (rough and direct, no sensitivities!) was used when dealing with an alcoholic. I knew all about that from past experiences with some people. Was Helen an alcoholic? I was not at all sure about that. Many times, when she telephoned me, I knew she had been drinking, but I explained it away to myself that the loss of her husband, whom Helen loved dearly, had temporarily placed her in a state of depression, and she took refuge in some pain-killing "medicine"—alcohol. Of course, I should have known better. But there had to be proof. How could I get proof when living a few hundred miles away?

If I failed to give her the message and something *would* happen to Helen due to excessive alcohol consumption, I would forever feel guilty. If I *did* give her the message—regardless of whether it was applicable or not—I would risk Helen's wrath, or disappointment in my judgment, or ridicule. But I knew that sooner or later I would have to tell her, in spite of the consequences. I decided it would have to be "later."

But now the phone call from Helen has revived the quandary. Again I decide the time to tell Helen is not now.

I divert myself by thinking about the man I married, the man who devoted his life to making me happy, by taking care of my children. What a personality he was!

He was the perfect example of a "pack rat"! He saved everything: screws, nails, pieces of wood, old toasters, radios, parts of engines, rusty tools, nonfunctioning fans and other sometimes unidentifiable machinery, paint cans with dried up and unusable paint residues, rocks from his geology days, books, drawings he had worked on a decade or more ago, a collection of forgotten and left-behind toys and little shoes from his children, notes from college and oil-field days, dozens of one-inch-long pencil remains of varying colors, and other items I couldn't even describe because their origin or purpose was so completely mysterious and indefinable. In the attic there were old glass bottles, a portable typewriter that seemed to be one of the first invented, numerous other strange-looking items, and boxes, boxes, boxes. But the boxes were *my* addiction, I have to admit.

When I had asked him one day why he was saving all this, he told me it came in handy when he needed something for repair or replacement; he wouldn't have to go to the store to buy it. I could never quite determine whether it was the miser within him or the time-saving aspect that prompted his collection.

He would not bat an eyelid if I spent one hundred dollars on a dress for myself or even bought a little frivolous item, but he would fight me tooth and nail for any dollar spent on the house. Once, after a heavy debate about the purchase of some curtains, I asked him (rather exhausted from the intense and rather infuriating discussion) why he would always put up so much opposition when in the end he would give in. "Well," he grinned, "it wouldn't be any fun to just let you go ahead and do what you want. After all, I want to have my say now and then, too." Then we both laughed.

Once, after his insistent stubbornness had brought me close to tears, I told him angrily, "You know, Bob, I love you—but right now I don't like you!"

He looked at me in surprise, without saying anything for a few moments. Then suddenly he laughed. "You know, honey, right now I don't like me, either! Forgive me?" He reached his hand over to me with an apologetic and mischievous grin.

It would test my patience that he would urge me to get ready for whatever appointment or date we had and then would be the one to linger—checking for burning cigarettes, open windows, and whatever else might strike his mind as a potential disaster lest it be thoroughly checked—while I was already sitting in the car waiting for him and trying not to let my temperature rise to the boiling point!

Most discussions we had were hardly ever without some form of intense debating. He loved to debate, to explain, to inform, to teach. Sometimes he would irritate me by the manner in which he would try to prove a point: teacher to pupil. I knew his superb knowledge and intelligence, but I didn't feel that I was stupid, either. "Don't act as though you were my father," I would flip back at him. "I'm your wife, remember?" But all our debates were based on and laced with respect and enthusiasm for each other's qualities.

For a moment I can feel myself getting weak. How can the pleasure of loving memories bring so much pain at the same time? O Bob! How could you do this to me? Die before I was ready to let you go? No warning? No preparation for death? Shouldn't everyone have the right for preparation? How could you do this?

And then sanity takes over again. How dare I think that we, the humans, have control. Bob died. Some day, so will I. It's only a matter of time. And time, in the context of eternity, is a very mysterious item within our mind.

But I know *one* thing; at some time or other, I shall be with Bob again.

In the meantime, I shall have to be satisfied with our conversation each evening.

I wonder what he'll tell me tomorrow.

12

New Concepts, Old Connections

O nce again, on our evening walk, Bob does come forth with a surprise. I asked him if we had been together in other lifetimes—and perhaps also with some of the people we know now in this lifetime.

"Oh, yes," he says casually, "there was a lifetime in Marseilles. You, Aline, and Frances were friends then. I believe it was in 1483."

I don't know why I didn't ask him more details about that, but instead went on to ask about Atlantis—perhaps because that subject had been a source of great debate between him and Frances. Bob claimed that, as a geologist, he knew much about the various layers of earth formation, he also knew enough about archaeological findings to know that should there have been such a continent, certainly one would be able to trace it to some degree, if with nothing else but artifacts from that time period. "There is absolutely not one item that would in any way, shape, or form indicate any such existence," he would vehemently declare. After such heated debate, on our way home I would argue with Bob over this, claiming that the possibility existed, that artifacts found in Egypt could have their origin in Atlantis, couldn't they? He couldn't quite refute the idea, but he also made it clear that he just didn't think so. His disbelief in the existence of Atlantis went as far as trying to prove his point by writing a letter to that extent to Frances, and she, in turn, responded with good arguments *for* the possibility of Atlantis's existence.

Bob enjoyed being "the devil's advocate." Perhaps that was the way he learned.

There were many other debates among Bob, myself, and a certain group of friends. One of the debates, again prompting Bob to write down his thoughts ("Lest I forget," he said) was a debate about Ruth Montgomery's statement in one of her books that she was told by a "guide" from the other side that one of her lifetimes had been during the reign of Tutankhamen. Bob tried vehemently to disprove that, with the result that Frances wrote him a letter with facts he had to accept. (Frances is a professor at a university and *has* to have her facts straight.)

I had glanced through some of his notes. I recognized that he was forever in conflict with the scientist within him in need of visible proof and the dreamer who wanted to believe that "faith is the substance of things hoped for, the evidence of things not seen." (Hebrews 11:1)

"We are here. Why are we here? We don't know. And we live out a span of years in association with our fellow humans—we propagate the race—we die. Does a part of this microscopic little being endure as a soul in space-time and go back and live many lives? Is there a structure, as described by some, with roles, cycles, levels, modes, etc., or are we not much more than a microscopic bacterial coating on a tiny ball spinning in space, caused by the fact that the ball has moisture and atmosphere," he wrote.

But among all debates the denial of Atlantis was the most vehement. Is that why I'm asking him now if perhaps we had a lifetime together in Atlantis?

To my utmost surprise he says, as though he had never doubted its existence, "Oh, yes. I was a perpetrator. You were a lady of honor."

I am so perplexed at this, and Hansi and I have arrived home by now, that I don't ask any further questions. I want to look up the two items *perpetrator* and *lady of honor* in the dictionary. What an odd expression! What could he mean by that?

At home I look up *perpetrator.* It's not a word I consciously remember having heard before. Bob had said it as though it were a term of address, like "Lady-in-Waiting" of the royal courts or such.

"Perpetrate: to perform, execute, or commit (something bad); to perpetrate a crime," the dictionary said.

As far as "Lady of Honor" goes, I cannot find any particular meaning. I'll have to draw my own conclusions.

Had Bob done something bad to me in Atlantean times? Did he want to forget about that and is that why he fought the idea of the existence of Atlantis so thoroughly? Does it matter for me to know? It's hard to imagine that in some lifetimes we may commit acts we're ashamed of now and would like to forget. Bob had said it too casually and without emotion—I decided it wasn't important. Out of curiosity I would like to know—just to *know.* But maybe now wasn't the time.

Time goes by. I have somewhat adjusted to my loss. The home improvements are finished. "Bendahouse" sparkles with newness and just enough change to preserve its original concept; I wanted to be sure it wouldn't lose any of its original personality.

The cemetery is not a place I have visited—what for? Physical remains are there, and they will disappear in time, become part of the earth. What is alive within and around me is much more important—and I have plenty of that! Perhaps I'm also afraid that being confronted with the visible reality of death will endanger my faith in the invisible which *does* remain: spirit and soul. It's not a case of refusing to accept reality (I have), but a refusal to expose myself willingly to more pain than I've already felt.

On my evening walks Bob has told me some very strange things—things that make me wonder if I'm not really making all this up. Some days ago I had asked him (out of curiosity for the answer) whether animals have a soul, too. His answer was, "Yes—they draw a limited supply of some kind of thought from the Universal Flow." When I asked him what that meant, he said that I should think about this myself and come up with my own answer. I could hear him chuckle. I went home and did some thinking about it, but felt rather dissatisfied since there was no one there who could tell me whether my thoughts were correct or not. Some day—some day, Bob, I argued angrily, I'll come back to you with something that'll baffle your mind!—at the same time fully aware of the ridiculous situation in which I had placed myself. I had to admit that Hansi, our German shepherd, did have a certain reaction to words, and I remembered that we had tested his vocabulary once (he responded to about eighty words). Of course, any loyal pet owner will swear to the existence of a soul of his/her particular pet—but receiving thoughts about "the Universal Flow"?! What *was* the Universal Flow, anyway? Could it be that thoughts really *were* concrete, like a flash of energy? And if so, were thoughts, like radio waves, sent into space, lingering or floating or finding a niche there? Now it was getting complex because this was going into physics. And that had not been my better subject in school! I put all these thoughts on hold for a while.

But tonight Bob really has come up with something that upsets me, although what he says is very nice. My question to him was prompted by a great feeling of gratitude: gratitude for twenty-two years of happiness, for my and his children and their love, for the rich and rewarding life I was allowed to lead while I was married to him, for the loyal and caring friends, for a loving family, the church I loved and became a part of because of him, for the beautiful house, and so on. As I had started on my walk, my heart was overflowing with gratitude instead of pain, and recognizing that elated me.

"Bob," I say, "there are so many people out there who are much better people than I am, who are lonely and without much love—how come I received so much? What have I done to deserve this kind of grace? In other words, why have I received so much, when there are so many good people who have not, who deserve it much more than I do?"

For a moment there is no answer from him. Then I hear this beloved chuckle: "You were touched by the star of Bethlehem," he says.

The answer almost angers me; is he making fun of me?

"Bob!" I'm sure my thoughts relay my irritation at this answer. "Bob! That's ridiculous!"

I believe my reaction has broken off the communication; besides, Hansi and I have reached home. I'm still irritated at this whole incident. But then I begin to think that perhaps I should take it seriously. If we do live more than one life, as some people believe, then perhaps I could have lived at the time of Jesus, and the hour of birth was perhaps taking place under the same stellar conditions. Well, whatever. I'm certainly not going to tell any of my friends about that. Maybe not even Aline and Frances, or Doris. They may think it rather funny. Ron, my son, would laugh and say teasingly,

"Mom, you *were* touched—but in your head," trying to make me laugh. As a matter of fact, I'm laughing a bit myself right now. Some months later, though, I will be forced to take another look at this.

My friends keep close and constant contact with me. Almost all of them know by now what is transpiring every evening on my walk with Hansi, and none of them seems to doubt the reality of my experience. I'm grateful for that and their friendship. Almost all of them give me books to read concerning such matters, and I'm learning more and more.

Naturally my mind is very much occupied. I am forced to bring to the surface the hidden patches of forgotten questions—those thoughts that were, in my younger years, in the process of trying to surface—but were placed right back from whence they came.

I have now begun to wonder *why* all this is happening to me. Is it part of God's immense love and grace for all humankind to have the ability to experience what I have? I have to believe that now. Yet, when I tell people my experiences and they ask me, "Why can't I have contact with my husband or wife or mother or father or child?"—any loved one departed—I don't have any really good answer. Somehow I sense there has to be a special connection among lives to bring about the continued connection. Could it be like a transmitter and a radio? The waves are being transmitted on a certain wavelength, but if the radio isn't turned on, the music can't be heard. How did I know to turn on the radio to the right wavelength? The answer is I *didn't*. It was sheer chance. My grief and pain were so severe that I had all my senses open to anything that would rescue me from that pain. Also, years ago, when Bob and I were discussing such matters, we had agreed that *if* such a thing were possible, whoever would leave the body first would try to contact the other partner to ease the pain.

Still, I'm sure some of our psychics know how to open that door and how to get contact.

It seems, then, that by a mere coincidence I became fortunate. Or did I? Am I supposed to tell my story in order for people to regain or broaden their faith in things unknown as yet to the human mind, to recognize that there is more than we dare hope for? That the grace of God perhaps surpasses all we've known so far?

For now I shall not continue these thoughts. Someday I shall have more answers.

Something strange happened this morning as I was taking Hansi for his morning walk. I heard Bob, for the first time since communication began, in the *morning!* That had never happened before, but I think it happened because of my dream last night.

The dream had very much upset me. It had to do with Bob, but it was not a happy dream; it disturbed me. Bob must have sensed my distress, for he told me not to pay too much attention to this particular dream, that there was an aspect to dreams hitherto unknown to us.

After my initial surprise (I was happy to hear Bob's voice after last night's dream experience), I asked him to tell me about that.

"Some dreams," he said, "are weak fragments from the universal flow, looking for a 'negative.' Some thoughts, as you well know, are sick or weak or even fragmented. When that happens, they do not find the right slot to go into and they wander around aimlessly, looking for a place to settle in or be dissipated."

"That," I said, "is, of course, assuming that I was right when I said, years and years ago, that thoughts were concrete—a concrete flow of energy. And as we know, energy can neither be created nor destroyed, right?"

"Yes, yes," he laughed, "you were right—as always!" And then he was serious again, "You see, everything, if it wants to work as a 'total,' needs a 'negative' and a 'positive,' and during sleep our brainwaves are a 'weak negative.' The

thought fragments (being 'weak positives') attach themselves to those 'weak negative' brainwaves, having found
their slot, because now they can be recorded and placed in
the proper slot as 'dreams.' "

Boy, oh, boy—that Bob! He really does it to me! Or am I
doing it to me?! Am I losing my mind? Before I have fully
comprehended what Bob has told me, he says, "You see,
everything in the universe runs in an orderly fashion. There
are no loose ends." With that his voice is gone, and I'm hur-
rying home to record what he told me, before I forget.

At home again, I quickly feed Hansi who is bugging me
for his morning meal, and then I record what I've heard.

After I've done that and read what it says, I am amazed; it
does seem to have some logic to it—but it's certainly what
some people would mockingly call "way out." Could I have
made up something like that? Perhaps—if I ever thought
about such things.

Today there was a call from Mae, Bob's youngest daughter, our little ballerina. She informs me that she'll be per-
forming in Miami—her dance troupe has an engagement
there to perform in October. She is very excited about it, and
so am I. There is no question in my mind; I shall go to Miami! It will be a bittersweet occasion. The last time I saw her
dance was with Bob in New York. At the same time I can
visit Helen and see if she's all right. Fort Lauderdale, where
Helen lives, is only a "cat's jump" away from Miami.

Filled with excitement, I plan my trip. Oh, how I love the
tropics! But even more so, I love to see my little darling
dance.

Before I know it, I'm in Miami.

I had rented a car in order to visit Helen and to get to the
theater. It's almost brand new and runs smoothly. Helen is
delighted to see me. We spend a pleasant few hours together, after I've cooked her a meal and we've eaten, and
then I leave to go back to the hotel. On the way back, the sky

is clouding up fast—one of the tropical thunderstorms is on the way. I have experienced them before—they never last long.

Suddenly it's dark as night, thunder and lightning are all around me, and the rain is pouring down in buckets, making visibility very difficult. I drive slowly and carefully.

Now, where do I turn left?

I'm on a highway, that's clear. But somewhere I have to turn left, to get to the beach to my motel.

Let's see—this street seems to be one to lead me there. The light is green and there is no car in sight; I turn left and proceed slowly to be able to read the street sign on my right. If only the rain would stop a little! It's so hard to read the sign with visibility close to zero.

Suddenly I hear a sound—the sound of screeching tires. I look to my right, and my heart stops a few beats; a car is coming toward me, trying to slow its speed so as not to hit me. But it will! I don't have enough speed to get out of the way! Oh, God, it's going to hit me!

All this has taken only seconds. My car is hit and spins around several times, until it faces the opposite direction from which I came when I faced the green light. Thank God, I think, thank God there's no car in front for me to collide with.

Then everything is at a standstill.

What's this trickling down my forehead? Blood. But it doesn't hurt.

There are people around me, asking if I'm hurt. I shake my head, and they look at me in a strange way, as though they don't believe that it doesn't hurt.

All I can think of is that Mae will be calling the motel to speak to me, and I won't be there. She'll be worried. I don't want her to worry. And I *am* going to see her dance, dammit!

"She'll need stitches," someone says. And then. "Are you sure you're all right? You're bleeding, you know. From the forehead."

There's a policeman. He looks at me and says, "I'm going to call an ambulance, ma'am. You've got to go to a hospital."

"No!" I say as vehemently as my condition permits. "No! I don't want to go to a hospital! I'm all right."

Mae. I've got to call her. I've got to get to a phone.

Someone directs me to a phone. I can't find a quarter for the phone call. Some kind person hands me a quarter. I recognize that I'm not in a wealthy neighborhood. Most of the people around me are of foreign descent, possibly Cuban. I'm deeply grateful for their help and kindness.

The message I leave for Mae is that I'll call her in the morning, and/or that I'll see her after the performance, as agreed. Now I feel better.

When I first wake up in the morning, I have a hard time remembering what happened last night. As I get up, I see myself in the mirror, and I don't know whether to laugh or cry. There's a huge white bandage covering my forehead at the hairline—it looks a lot like a fashionable headband, Olivia Newton style!

I have to hurry if I want to make it in time to the performance. I call a taxi. At the theater, I find my seat and have time to look around me. The theater is packed full, not one single seat available except one—the one next to me!

The one where Bob would sit, if he were here with me, today.

Coincidence?

After the performance, after finding Mae, she hugs me first and then says, "What happened?" I laugh, "The newest style for headgear!"

After I've told her what happened, she's glad and relieved that I'm all right. It took eighteen stitches, but they'll disappear in time.

We have two more wonderful days.

On the plane, I reflect back to the past two days. I still see Mae sitting at the beach, red reflections radiating from her hair in the sun, her lithe body practicing for the next performance; I remember our talks and the sharing of feelings and thoughts and stories; having dinner together in the charming hotel restaurant and suddenly hearing a conversation in German from the next table; our ride back in the taxi with more talk, more shared feelings, being so close . . . and then the good-by. And I still feel the lump in my throat each time I have to let my husband's children go away from me and telling myself they're only away in body, not in spirit.

These were days to build memories again—now it's back to my familiar realities. There are many of them waiting for me, but I'm always glad to be back home: my life is there. There's Hansi; and Jezebel, the cat; and the squirrels; and the birds; and the raccoons; my family; and my Bob.

But again I notice something puzzling: the plane seat next to me is *also* empty, as had been the seat in the otherwise fully packed theater.

For a moment I think I feel Bob's presence.

13

Sight of That Immortal Sea

"Though inland far we be,
our souls have sight of that immortal sea
Which brought us hither."

—Wordsworth

"Would you want coffee or tea?" I ask Aline and Frances. They've come to hear the tape.

They both decide on coffee, which I place before them, and then I put the tape in the recorder. This is the first time after the hypnosis session that I'm letting us, including myself, hear what was recorded by Carl Schlotterbeck during my attempted "stop-smoking" hypnosis—an event that turned out to be something quite different.

"Since it doesn't take two hours to tell me that smoking is bad for me," I had smiled at Carl Schlotterbeck, the hypnotherapist, "maybe instead you could try something out on me. There was an incident some years ago that left me wondering," and I told him about the reincarnation SIG "regression" session, where I saw the strange mountain range, which I later thought I had identified as Massada. Carl had agreed. He concentrates his therapy mostly on past-life regression. He found that it was worthwhile exploring the possibility of interaction of past-life experiences with current life events, possibly interfering with proper functioning of mind and emotions. He had been quite successful in some cases.

I didn't feel that I needed therapy any more than any other human being (everyone can benefit from therapy), but then, no one can ever know what may lie hidden in the unconscious mind. In this instance, I just wanted to find out what could have been the cause for my utter distress and pain in seeing the people walk along that mountain range.

From my previous, and first, session with Carl I knew that he was able to hypnotize me. I remembered that it had been a pleasant experience, and so I was quite relaxed as he started.

Now, back at my house again, the three of us are anxiously waiting to hear what took place. I had told Carl very little about the Massada incident—I wanted no influence.

We're listening to Carl's voice: soothing, comforting, deep, rich, with a gentle but strong resonance.

"And you recall these images and those feelings," we hear him say. There is a long pause. For a while we hear nothing; it seems I'm taking my time, trying to concentrate.

"... to what, indeed, begins to come to memory ... " I hear him continue.

Another long pause.

Then, in a subdued, slightly heavy voice, I hear myself say, "I'm trying to recapture it ... " Pause.

"What does come?" His voice is so soothing.

"It's very difficult for me ... It's so strange; when I'm at home, alone, I see it, and now I find it difficult to get it back . . . " I recognize my voice, yet it's somewhat different: slower, heavier.

"What do you see when you're at home, alone?"

"When I try to picture the scene?"

"Yes."

"Okay . . . " It's obvious I'm still restrained. Something inside of me is fighting recognition. Pause. Then, slowly, "People, walking, across from me . . . I'm on a mountain. The mountain is not all that high, I would say, in comparison to the size of the people, from where they're walking. It's about the size of ten people down and the size of ten people up." Strange comparison! "To the right, the sky, not very bright blue, just kind of like a light gray, but the sun, I think, is shining; it's not dark." Pause. "People are walking . . . " Pause.

"Fast or slowly?"

"Slowly. Heavy . . .You know, it goes up a little bit, and then it goes down, and then it goes up again. It's a very slim path, I know that, even though I can't see that far. And they're all dressed in dark clothes. I don't see anything bright there . . . 'course, that could be because they're so far away. They all seem to have some dark clothes on." I sound almost puzzled. "Strangely enough, I do not capture any feelings right now . . . and I'm wondering 'why not?' "

"If you did—what would be there? . . . the feelings that you recall, as you recall . . . "

"I have to try to recapture what I first felt when I first saw it . . . " My voice again is heavy, strained. Pause. "Can't capture it . . . But I remember what I felt when I first saw it . . . There was pain as if . . . they were looking for help. But they hadn't found it yet."

Aline and Frances sit quietly. No one says a word. Listening to the tape, I'm amazed at the fluctuation of my voice: from easygoing to heavy and subdued, to whispering, to peppy, to puzzled.

"And so, while they were walking, I could feel what they

were feeling." My voice is very matter-of-fact at that statement. "It wasn't anything specific, just a feeling . . . I don't
understand why I can't capture the feeling . . . " Frustration
in my voice. "It's just a memory—but there is no *feeling*
there . . . "

Now Carl's voice comes to me. "When you did feel it,
where inside of you did you feel it?"

"It was in my heart." The way I pronounce the word *heart*
is so strange. It doesn't sound like me at all.

"And as best as you can recall, what did it feel like in your
hear?"

"I wanted to cry. And I did." I say it like a child recalling a
bad experience and then later on telling people about it. "I
don't know how to describe it in any other way." Now it's my
voice again.

"That's all right. Now just tell me the first thing that ap-
pears when I ask you this about that feeling: if words . . . if
that wanting to cry, if there were tears there that would want
to be said, what does it feel like you would have wanted to
have said?"

"There's help . . . And that I can feel with them, and that
there's hope, that the journey isn't all that much longer . . .
it's right around the mountain . . . " Long pause.

"And at that vantage point, from which you see them . . . I
want you to focus all your attention to the point from where
you're observing them."

"The hill is a mountainous area behind me. I'm standing
on something like a path that they're standing on . . . that
they're walking on, except on the other side . . . " Until now
my voice has been casual. Now I can hear it slowing down
again, with a trace of emotion in it. "I can feel something
now . . . I have a long, white dress on, and a belt, and either
I'm barefoot, or I have sandals. And I carry something in my
right hand. It's light, but I don't know what it is . . . " And now
my voice, as if triumphant over the recognition, "It's like a
little pouch! I don't know what's in it."

"Just be aware of the feeling of it."

"There's a breeze blowing." That came quickly.

"From what direction is the breeze blowing?"

Again the answer comes very fast. "To the right—*from* the right, I mean. I must have long hair. It's blowing in the wind." Pause. And then, with subdued traces of emotion, "I wonder if they're thirsty . . . " Pause. Then, almost a whisper, as though talking to myself, "It's very frustrating that I can't get to them."

"Yes," Carl says, with sympathy. "What does that frustration there do to you?"

"It upsets me." The upset is apparent in my voice.

"I want you to focus on that upset, just the feeling of it . . . " Pause.

Carl continues, "If there's something you'd like to do or want to say . . . "

"Well, I'd like to go to them, but by the time I get there, they'll all be gone . . . because it's a long walk down the hill and across the ravine, up the hill, and by that time they will have reached Jesus." Small pause. "And besides, I'm not sure that's the only reason . . . maybe I'm just afraid of the long walk." Pause. "But I think . . . I think . . . what I find difficult, is this: when I saw this the first time in my vision or reliving it or whatever it is . . . " my voice is very matter-of-fact. It's obvious I'm fighting hard *not* to remember. " . . . it ended right there. And now that you ask me what I would do, I wonder why it didn't continue my first time. Why did it stop right there? Oh, I know, I remember now: 'cause I started crying, and the guide was supposed to get people out of it." I'm referring, of course, to the regression session at home when Bob was still alive among us. "So now I have to re-evaluate the question anew, from a different aspect, a different continuation of it." Still very matter-of-fact, fighting it all the way! "But I have to get the feeling first." As though by not getting the feeling back, I'll be saved from remembering.

"Do you?"

"I did, for a while there. And now it's gone again."

"What was there, when you had it?"

"Sadness . . . " Pause.

"When you were standing there on that hill with that sadness inside, what . . . "

"Yeah, but you know," I hear myself interrupt him, "something else is coming through; I just had the feeling that those who had reached Jesus were doing all right." I sound almost relieved. "So it was just a matter of the others making it to that point. And that does make me feel good." It's also very apparent in my voice. Pause. "I wonder, why I, as I grew older, when I learned about Jesus, well, *really* learned about him—we had religion classes in school and we were graded on it—I learned about it when I was ten, eleven, twelve years old, during that time"—my voice is my everyday, "current" voice—"and I could very much identify with him. Actual feelings"—with emphasis on "feelings." "I could sometimes feel what he felt, and I thought that was a little bit unusual that I lost it as I grew older, that personal close feeling. It was more a matter of my intellect taking over and it had become *learned;* well, at first it was very, it was almost, I would say it was almost like a memory." Here I can hear myself saying it in an almost embarrassed little chuckle, almost apologetic. "But . . . I don't know . . . it was just very intense." All the time I have the feeling I'm trying to place my emphasis on the reality, the security of reality, of this lifetime—all, so that I won't have to remember. "And at that regression session, you know, the incident with the people walking, the first time that feeling had come back. It was close, anyway. There was a connection there, that I hadn't recognized before until just now." Boy. Oh, boy: am I trying hard to stay away from the real issue! Carl seems to know it, too. He wants to get on, instead of hearing all my attempts at rationalization! I hear it from his several "hmm, hmm's."

Carl is trying to get me back on track. "Yeah," he says, "and that feeling of closeness, you can recall what that was like when you were young, that feeling . . . "

Without hesitation a very firm, determined "yes" from me.

Carl seems to be looking for another reattachment point.

" . . . and you can recall whether you have the feeling emotionally or not, when you did have the feeling—how did you feel inside?"

"A *lot* of different feelings . . . " I hear myself say this with profound emphasis. "I recognized, I don't know whether in words or just in feeling, at that age already, that . . . the reason for the need for Jesus' living and dying. And it just about overwhelmed me. I recognized that man is man is man and needs to have someone," I can hear suppressed tears and pain in my voice, "who will uplift him and forgive and guide. And what hurt me was that when Jesus died, he still could only love, because humanity didn't even recognize it." The tears are now openly displayed in my voice. "Then. They didn't recognize it." There's a sniffle. "Or some did. But why didn't all? I just didn't *want* him to die."

"You just what?"

"I didn't want him to die. I wish he would have continued living. I mean, why did death have to be involved? But, of course, there is the resurrection, and one has to recognize," I hear myself sniffle again, "the physical form disappears, but what was there as the vital part stays. And survived quite a few thousand years." Pause.

"Let's return to that feeling: 'I did not want him to die.' I wish for you to be aware that your subconscious mind has already connected you in with something. I wish for you to repeat that phrase and connect you with when you first said that: 'I did not want him to die.' "

"I did not want him to die," I hear myself say, with my voice expressing such emotional pain that even listening to the tape after the session, I get caught up in this inner upheaval.

"Again."

"I did not want him to die." Now the tears are coming through more strongly.

"Again."

"I did not want him to die." Now there's sad resignation.

"The next thing that comes to you."

"Well, the connection to my husband, of course. But the original part of that was Jesus. My husband had nothing to do with that. But I put in the connection from Jesus to now . . . Quite a big jump, isn't it?" I seem to be laughing under tears, trying to conceal my pain.

"Now let your subconscious mind give you the scene where you first said that: 'I did not want him to die.' "

"Yes." There's no hesitation now. Where before words came rather slowly, they're now coming fast. "He walked to the cross." Now I'm not hearing myself say anything, just the sounds of subdued crying.

"What's coming to you?"

"I can't stop it." Again the pain in my voice, trying not to cry, affects me, listening to myself relating something that I seem to have witnessed such a long, long time ago. There's a pause, I hear myself openly sobbing now. "I can't even help carry the cross." All this is said with subdued sobs. I'm crying.

"What's that do to you in there, inside?"

"It makes me a little angry, too." My voice shows a mixture of pain, anger, restrained frustration. It's obvious I'm trying to regain composure, because now the voice shows an attempt at the usual rationalizing casualness. "I'm trying to figure out what I can do"—still trying to stop crying.

"How close are you to seeing this?" Pause. "What do you see there?"

"It's . . . it's . . . a very sandy road . . . I'm . . . they're there, and I'm here . . . and there's the crowd. I'm right among the crowd . . . " I'm still crying, still trying to stop my sobs . . . "It's pretty dusty and hot . . . I just don't want to see it." That last sentence is said with composure regained.

"Yeah . . . What does it do to you to see it?"

"It tears me up." Pain in my voice. Under sobs, "And yet, you know, I can't . . . Barabbas . . . I can't wish that instead he die—I don't want anybody dead . . . " Still crying. Pause. Then, "He must be thirsty . . . " Pause. Then, with a mixture of pain, frustration, and anger, "And I can't even give him a drink of water!" Now more intense sobbing.

"Let the tears come," Carl says softly.

My sobbing gets more intense: "Not even that! That really makes me angry . . . and it hurts . . . " More crying.

"If you could have spoken what was in your heart there, what would you have said?"

"Stop it! You don't know what you're doing!" More angry, frustrated, crying.

"And then?"

"I don't know . . . I don't know. I don't remember what I did . . . " This is said with resigned pain. "I don't know whether I stayed around and cried or whether I went home . . . " Trying to control my sobs.

"What's the last clear thing?"

Silence. Still trying to stop crying. "The last clear thing . . . There's a doorway . . . but not modern, of course, it's almost like . . . I don't know if it's straw or something . . . it's something like a hut or so . . . but . . . I don't know why I would be in a hut there . . . I don't know what they had in those days." My composure seems to have been regained.

"That's all right. Just describe it."

"But it's a bit more shady and cooler in there. There isn't really any furniture or anything in it . . . nothing that I can remember. I'm just in there . . . I have a . . . I have a scarf on, a white scarf . . . with a knot in the back . . . and I'm lying down on the ground with my two hands like this underneath my head. It's pretty hard there—the sand is stamped down, you know, it's not dusty. It's hard yellow sand, and I feel pretty sick . . . nauseated . . . I need to drink, but I don't want to because *he* didn't have anything to drink . . . and I'm getting more nauseated . . . " Long pause. Sighs.

"What do you feel is happening in your body as you become more nauseated?"

"I feel better now . . . it's gone, I feel better already. I don't know why . . . " Pause. "Maybe it's done, and I know he's really living . . . " Now, as if in a daze, I continue. "There's a red sun . . . a real red sun . . . how a sun can be so red . . . funny thing is that star: it's always been there . . . to the left of the sun . . . and how can the sun and the star be visible at the same time . . . I don't know . . . it doesn't make any sense . . . but if I would describe it, the star is about at ten o'clock to the left of the sun, and . . . I would say, in vision, how shall I describe the distance . . . it's hard to describe it . . . well, if the sun would be two feet of the right of me, it would be five feet above me. I mean in vision . . . and two feet to the left. Like here's the sun, and the star is there . . . but that doesn't make any sense . . . not when it's the sun . . . I don't think it was the moon . . . "

"That's all right . . . " Carl soothes. I think he knows I'm trying to avoid a vision of something else . . .

Deep breaths. Silence.

"I don't know what to do with myself now . . . "

"That's all right . . . I want you to go back into some of those other memories, either on the hillside or with the crowd . . . or in the hut. Just whatever comes back to you, spend just a few more minutes . . . seeing a little more there . . . you might be aware of that long white dress, and that belt that you had there . . . even putting it on . . . "

"Funny—I didn't wear a scarf then." My voice is back to normal. "I had a different outfit there than I did downhill on the street." Pause . . . "I don't want to think about that street scene . . . " My voice is becoming tearful again. "It upsets me . . . but on the hill, that doesn't so much . . . I think . . . "

"What's the difference? What's the difference that makes that hillside okay?"

"Well, Jesus was alive. And I know that there was help there. But you know, it doesn't make any sense either, because . . . I mean . . . if I believe in the resurrection, then it doesn't matter whether his physical form dies, but . . . "

"That's all right," Carl interrupts, "but you didn't quite know that then."

"Yeah, I guess so. But it felt good. I think I wanted to go and see him myself. I don't think I had seen him or met him, when I was standing on the hill. But I *knew* about him, and maybe *had* seen him once, I'm not sure, but I just didn't know him that well, and I knew of him and knew what he could do."

"And you liked that, didn't you ?"

"Uh-huh."

"And you had obviously seen something that would *make* you like that."

"Yeah," that sounds almost surprised, a memory slowly reentering . . .

Carl continues: "Something about life, about the people? . . . "

My voice, searching, "Yeah . . . "

Carl: "That made you appreciate very specially what he did for them . . . "

I, searching again: "I have to . . . think . . . I get . . . I get some inkling . . . " Pause. My voice is very subdued again. "I was sitting down . . . at the mountain . . . and he was sitting . . . and he was sitting . . . I was sitting here with a lot of people . . . and he was up here, and there was the end of the top of a mountain . . . " Pause.

Carl: "What's it like to be there?"

My voice is filled with subdued, but overwhelming admiration, awe . . . "Oh, it's very special . . . I couldn't believe it . . . it makes me want to cry, too, would you believe it?"

"Uhuh . . . "

"He has something very special," the voice still reflects that overwhelming sense of awe, "my God . . . the *power* . . . " This is whispered, almost inaudible, "And the strength that radiates . . . I know I will never forget it . . . I will *never* . . . forget it . . . " Pause. Then, still in a whisper, "I would like to remember what he is telling us . . . " Pause. Then, a little louder again, " . . . love thy neighbor as thyself . . . " Pause. "And I can identify with that." My voice is now normal again. "Because I haven't always done that. I had heard of some people, and I didn't really like them . . . I don't know if I considered them 'neighbors' . . . funny I should have called my cat 'Jezebel,' because 'Jezebel' was the name of one of them." I'm chuckling a little, bringing past and present together without any concern, " . . . but my cat Jezebel is very nice. And I found that I was judging too quickly." My voice is almost back to my present-time voice, it's now very alert and relaxed. "But the thing is, I didn't have to feel bad about me. It was not . . . He never said anything that made me feel bad. When he said it, it was total love. And I could accept it because of that. There was never any criticism." Pause, then, with clear firmness: "He reached my intellect as well as my soul." Pause. Suddenly I'm sobbing again: "And . . . I have to get back to that scene . . . " Pain, angry frustration, sobbing.

"Which scene?"

"The one on the road, the cross . . . " still sobbing.

"Something has happened that made you aware that you have to get there," Carl prompts. "Something you've heard, you've seen, that makes you need to get there . . . "

"I don't want to remember . . . " I'm sobbing. The pain in my voice and in my sobs is unmistakable: there is a memory I want to forget . . .

"Someone has told you something . . . "

I make a sound indicating I want to end my sobbing, a sort of sigh, trying to regain composure. Then, slowly and with resigned disappointment: "Of all people . . . a friend of Barabbas . . . " I'm still trying not to cry again, trying to control my sobs. "I don't remember what it was he told me. I was so upset . . . and then I just really couldn't believe it, either."

I'm still trying to get control. Tears are still audible in my voice. "I tell you, if I would not be so upset over it, I would believe I'm making all this up . . . but I don't think so . . . and . . . " I'm sobbing again; there are no words for a while. Carl is encouraging, "Yes?"

I continue as though now resigned that I *have* to remember . . . "But I remember what he looked like . . . it was a 'he' who told me . . . he did have a beard, and he did have a turban. Kind of turban, I don't know. Some kind of headgear that looked like a turban. And he wore . . . a tan leather vest. And . . . I don't know . . . he may have been barefoot . . . " Pause. Then there is something I can't understand on the tape. My voice is not sounding like my normal voice. Long pause. "I think . . . I think . . . he told me almost in mockery . . . " Now I sound as though I've brought my emotions under control. Sigh. "It doesn't bother me." I seem to be back in control over my emotions. "What is this . . . " Pause. "That's why I don't want to remember the words."

"Okay," Carl says, soothingly. "Okay, there's no need to. Do recall again, sitting on the hillside, when he was there, when his presence was there, physical . . . " Long pause. "You can see and hear . . . you can feel that power that indeed you have remembered . . . "

"It's not there now."

"The *memory* is . . . If you could have spoken to him, then, there, knowing what you know now, what would you have liked to have been able to have said to Him?"

After a few seconds, "I don't want to say it, but it's there . . . except . . . I think it's just a phrase . . . I was going to say, 'I will follow you till the end of my days' . . . but I think I've heard that phrase, I'm just using that."

"That's all right. What else would you like to say to him?"

"That . . . I must agree with what he said: that love is the most powerful, the most important thing in life . . . love does conquer all . . . that's what he said, of course. These three things about love: love conquereth all . . . I forget what it was

... love beareth all, love understandeth all ... and that ... he wanted to be sure that when all the other things about him were said, and there were many important things, and we would hear many important things, and a lot of it would be quoted slightly different, and that wouldn't matter. The main thing was to remember *that* ... And that, if we could do that, we would never have to worry about anything, that that was the total message. Everything else around it was just learning and passing on, so that people would find it easier to live. And that's really when I felt the beginning of understanding what he was in for. I think I had an inkling of what was going to happen. I knew that when I ... it wasn't so much what he said—it was his *presence* ... the presence was something that would frighten some people. He really *could* have been king of the world. He had the presence to it—or for it or whatever. But I think what frightened them most was the fact that he *didn't* ... it was something they couldn't understand. I wanted to learn more, but I was needed somewhere else, I don't really know for doing what, I think nursing someone ... " Then, after a short pause, drained, exhausted, "I'm very tired. I don't really want to remember any more."

"Okay. I want you to be aware of that tiredness coming from there, too, probably at the end ... want you to come to the very end of that life ... want you to begin to disconnect from that physical body ... and how the end comes to you ... every move that comes there ... " Long pause. "What's it like to leave that behind ... "

My voice, quite clear, not sleepy as before, "I haven't gone through the process of actually leaving it physically behind—I jump quickly, I guess. Maybe because there are other things, unpleasant ... I don't know, but I know the feeling of *being* away from it ... and it's a nice feeling, because ... I don't know if this is now my belief in reincarnation, but I'm learning, even on the other side. And that makes me feel good to be able to do that. Because I didn't feel I had learned enough from Jesus. I *really* don't feel I'd learned enough. So I feel I have to catch up. Still, I don't think I did all that much catching up in other lives . . . except this one." I seem to be back at the present. "I *did* catch up, this time."

"Yeah . . . as you would leave that body," Carl is still probing (as I found out later on, with an insight into more), "why don't you just take the first thoughts that occur to you when I ask you this: you were reasonably close to him . . . in time and space then . . . heard some of his teachings . . . what you thought was most important, as you look back on that life, perhaps even get some memories of growing up, seeing the people, knowing what they would be getting from him, because *you* knew what they would get, and then seeing him treated that way . . . seeing him actually die, what do you think he would have said to you?"

There is a short pause. Then, with slow, deliberate, precise pronunciation: "I . . . am . . . doing . . . what . . . must . . . be done . . . what is happening is something that has to happen **and** you must recognize that . . . " Pause. "That my physical form is not important—what I *taught* you is. And that there *is* life eternal." That last part is said almost casually, with great simplicity. "And that I should not be so 'earthbound' . . . but think more thoroughly about what he taught, and if I would *really* understand it, then I wouldn't feel sad . . . and upset." Pause. Then, with seemingly comfortable emotions, "He said, 'The greatest power on earth and the greatest strength on earth is . . . contained in the phrase . . . "Love thy neighbor as thyself." ' And that not many people can master that fully. But if they *can,* then nothing can hurt them. And that I should think about that of my own and add my *own* thoughts to that. And I don't know if I've ever done that. I've never even *thought* about it until just now." Long pause.

The first side of the tape ends here.

I flip over to the next side. By now I've listened to it only a few times—with great intervals. Listening to it drains me, and yet, after some time has passed and I find myself playing it to a few special people, I get caught up in it again.

Sometimes, when I take a walk along our small, old country road, I try to repeat in my mind some of the sentences from the tape, trying to evaluate whether the obvious emotional turmoil contained in it will surface. But even when I think of Bob's passing to the other side—an obvious introduction to sadness and grief—there are no feelings that can come even close to those which I hear and feel listening to my voice on the tape.

I know that Carl is convinced that what I experienced was a very real past-life memory. But am I?

Before I turn the tape player back on, I ask Frances and Aline if they would want to hear the other side some other time. To be honest, I would prefer that—I'm tired. Listening to the tape drains me.

They both feel the same way, and we decide to continue listening a few days from now. For tonight we have a lot to discuss, to analyze, to debate.

After they've left, I rush to get to bed. I feel as though I need to sleep for two full days.

14

Two Solitudes

"Love consists in this, that two solitudes protect and
touch and greet each other."

—Rainer Maria Rilke

Although I can still feel the strain from yesterday's
"past-life regression" session, I dare indulge myself in
memories. Or maybe they just came along. Or maybe
there's more to the experience than I let myself remember,
and my mind, my psyche, is searching for a way to escape
the memory of something apparently very painful from a
long, long time ago by replacing it with a happy memory of
not so long ago.

In any case, I have decided to enjoy what is being offered
to me today: a taste of nature abundantly overflowing with
beauty. Now and then a glimpse of scenes revealed in the
tape recording want to force their way into my mind, but I

push them aside; not today, tomorrow.

Instead I let the sunshine saturate me and I turn myself over to the gift of life.

Until now I have not been able to look at any photograph showing Bob's beloved face—the need for his physical presence would immerse me in a shock wave of pain.

But for some reason, today I permit myself one small taste of a memory, like a diabetic trying out one dose of sugar, afraid of the consequences, yet compelled to indulge just this once.

Sometime ago, sensing springtime in the air, Bob and I had been sitting on the patio, as I am today.

All the wild little creatures around us had started reacting to the signals of the season: squirrels and chipmunks scurrying around, birds flying back and forth to their nests, jonquils shyly peeking through the protective cover of the earth, and first buds of life appearing on the trees and shrubbery.

Bob and I were filled with contentment. The hauntingly sweet music of *Summertime* filled the air and lingered within our hearts.

"God, I love that music," Bob had said. "It reminds me so much of the South." He had been born and spent his first five years of life in New Orleans. We were planning to visit there after his retirement. Now . . . no! I will not think about that! I shall think about what *was*—not about what could be.

I had looked over at him while the music was playing; he looked so relaxed and happy, healthy and suntanned and handsome—and I felt so lucky. We were compatible; my temperament, which could at times be rather explosive, had become much calmer since I had been married to him; all the rough edges had smoothed out.

A feeling of total happiness and comfort surrounded me like a cozy, soft blanket: emotional velvet. I gave myself to that feeling without restraint—and why not? Forgotten were all the turmoils of the first part of my life; life was here and now, with Bob, and Bendahouse, and the children visiting (his and mine), and the wildlife, and trees and shrubs and flowers, and the seasons changing and ever renewing: life in action. Forever.

I had gone over to where Bob was sitting and hugged him passionately. "I love you. I love this place. I love this country. I'm part of all that. You're the most important."

Slightly taken by surprise, he laughed good-naturedly. "My God—what brought that on? Here I'm getting worried because you have that absent-minded look on your face— and with you, always full of surprises, one never knows— and then you come and attack me with passion."

I laughed along with him, "Ah, well, maybe it's because it's spring. Springtime is so pretty."

"And so are you."

"And you're wonderful."

"Mutual Admiration Society," he grinned.

"Right. And why not?"

"All right, since you're in such a generous mood, why don't you put one of your German tapes on. The other one is 'fini.' "

I complied with his request, all the while counting my blessings.

Perhaps, once in a while, we are fortunate and blessed enough to capture, if only for a few sacred moments, a glimpse of eternity.

"I viewed the world with loving eyes
And captured
A glimpse of Paradise —
Enraptured ... "

The German classic, Goethe's words, which I had not thought about for years, suddenly found its way back into my heart.

Now here I am.

And my Bob . . . well, I shall have to concentrate on thoughts. Thank God for thoughts. Thank God for memories.

But now I have to be very, very careful. Memories, if indulged in at the wrong moment, for too long a time, can be a dagger. And it's too beautiful a day to let daggers destroy.

By thinking about Bob, my mind returns my thoughts back to another time not too long ago.

During the first hypnosis—the time when I just wanted to find out if I *could* be hypnotized—there appeared to have been a past-life memory. It seems that I was placed in a time period of 1648 (I stated the year during the session), and I saw myself walking across a very small wooden bridge toward a mansion. After having crossed the bridge, I walked on a sandy path, past small Tudor-style houses, toward a mansion. I wore a loose, long blue skirt with a pretty apron, a blouse (I believe it was white or light yellow), and I was barefoot. I had waited for a while, waiting for a lover who hadn't come. To the left of me was a meadow running along the stream, to the right of me were the houses.

I neared the mansion; it had large white pillars at the entrance, and I had my room upstairs in the attic with a small window looking down on the meadow. There was a mattress of straw, but it had sheets. I went down into what was called a "washroom" to do the wash. That was done in a big tub with a washing board—much as they were still in existence in Europe at the turn of and into the early part of the twentieth century.

Apparently I was what was called a scullery maid.

Other than that there had been a flock of geese toddling along the path before I got to the mansion. There was no other incident; nothing happened. It was just like a quick visual scene from a movie.

Then the scene changed.

Now I was on my way toward a ship, lying at anchor in

the harbor. The ship was a sailing vessel, but rather large for those days. I remember walking down into a cabin to meet my husband, who was the captain of the ship. Wooden stairs led down into the cabin, which was rather dark. As I climbed down the steps, a man was approaching, but I don't think it was my husband. It was not the captain. Again, nothing happened, and the scene was finished.

Then Carl asked me a question about my death in that particular lifetime. Apparently, according to my voice on the tape, "There was something wrong with my legs, from the knee down . . . varicose veins or something."

After he had suggested to me to "leave that physical body behind and move further and further away from it," I say, after a long pause and then almost in a whisper, " . . . a veil, a golden veil . . . like a wing around you . . . like a cocoon . . . " and, with what seems like amusement, " . . . it puts you in a cocoon . . . " Then, serious again, "That golden veil . . . but it feels good."

Now Carl says, with his deep, gentle, soothing voice, "And that golden veil, that moves you where?"

"All around: left and right, up and down, nowhere in particular, just moving. And I don't like that. Except, of course, it feels good. But I don't like moving around like that. I wish it would go to just one place."

"But it actually does," Carl continues.

"Perhaps."

"Somewhere there, there's a great light."

After a pause on the tape again, I hear myself saying, "Well, I'm not sure whether the veil wasn't a light. It just felt like a veil, you know. But . . . that's very strange . . . right now I can see only one color; it's a very intense, luminous blue."

"What does it feel like?"

"Not much of anything. I'm just very curious. I've still got that veil around me, so I feel protected. And I don't know why I think I *need* protection; this blue thing isn't very frightening. It's just . . . I don't know what it is."

"Is it comfortable?"

"It's not uncomfortable."

"Is the veil comfortable?"

"Yes." I say that with emphasis. "It feels, you know, very secure and warm. And it isn't confining, it gives way to every movement."

After that Carl guides me back to present reality again. Aline and Frances accompanied me home, but we were all tired and didn't discuss the tape's content until a later time.

I hadn't been too impressed with any of this—there was no emotional response in either one of these "visions"— that's all I'm inclined to call them. I felt I could have seen any of these scenes in a movie, and my mind was identifying this with a so-called "past-life memory."

That was, until my evening walk with Hansi.

Naturally, I told Bob about this, and that, *if* it happened to have been a past-life memory, the two scenes were possibly related.

He agreed to having been the ship's captain and my husband, but mentioned nothing about the "scullery maid" scene. During the conversation—in a question-and-answer mode—he told me that he drank all of his money away, and since I was left alone for much of the time, with little money, I had taken on a lover, whom he killed. That happened before he took his ship past the Cape of Good Hope, where it sank in a storm.

Well, that was quite a story! I decided that I always knew I had a good imagination (after all, I *am* a writer!), and I placed this whole episode into the category of "overactive imagination."

Nevertheless, I looked up in the *World Book Encyclopedia* whether it was possible for ships in 1648 to sail that far around the world to the Cape of Good Hope. I didn't even know whether ships like that existed at that time. I felt embarrassed to admit to myself my lack of knowledge, but consoled myself with the thought that everybody has some weak points and some strong points.

What I found in the encyclopedia startled me.

There were drawings of different types of early sailing ships and, without looking for their names or types, I picked one that resembled what I had seen, just by the shape. Then I read what it said: it was called a "caravel."

I looked up "Christopher Columbus"—I believe because it referred to that in the information given. (Again: my knowledge of time in historic events was and is limited.)

In gathering all this information, it became quite clear that a sailing ship (or caravel) could have sailed past the Cape of Good Hope, toward Capetown in South Africa.

I should have asked him what the name of the ship was, but I was too anxious to go home to look up the missing information. The next evening there were other items of interest discussed.

However, I now am no longer sure that all of this was created by my imagination. What really startled me was that there were twelve different types of early sailing vessels, and I had immediately picked one that looked like the one I had been on during the session. I had found it difficult to describe its appearance when Carl asked me to do so, but had no trouble at all identifying it when I saw it.

Now, thinking back to that experience, questions arise again: do I really believe in the possibility of living more than one life?

I ponder over this for quite some time.

And then, finally, I'm able to put it into one phrase: *Life is one continuous flow of energy, indestructible, that may appear in various forms and existence, either individually or collectively connected, or both, throughout eternity.* (By "connected" I mean "coming from the same source and returning there.")

If, by chance, the energy field surrounding and connected to human beings should contain the same genetic information as DNA on the *physical* level, then that could also apply to the invisible, the intangible information concerning "soul" material; that certain information, differing with each individual soul, is transmitted from lifetime to lifetime in different physical form. That could also apply to certain memory factors.

Of course, while all these observations are interesting, they're not all that important; what's more important is the fact of life itself and the memory of origin and destination. Once I asked a friend, who is an established author and lecturer on various topics, including that of reincarnation, whether he believed in reincarnation. He answered, "When I'm asked that question, I give only one answer: 'Reincarnation is not something to believe in—it's something to know about.'"

Gloria calls. She wants to know how I am. I tell her I'm all right.

"Have you heard from Greg lately?" she asks.

"I got a phone call two days ago—from Florida."

"Really?" she sounded surprised. "How is he?"

"Well, he claims he has a nice job, is going to college, has a nice girl friend, etc., etc. You know, the usual reassurance lie. That's what I call it."

"You didn't buy it."

"Of course not. But I still feel sorry for him."

"You have too much compassion, Mother," she says with slight reproach. "And sometimes that's a bit misplaced, you know."

I had to smile; it was *she* who approached us first to ask if we could help Greg. He was just released from a mental hospital, had no place to go, faced a court trial for charges his father had placed against him, and would end up on the street as a "homeless" unless someone offered him shelter.

"Don't worry, honey"—not much sense mentioning all this—"don't worry; Dad and I weren't the kind that wanted to go out and save the world—you know that. Not that there isn't some merit in that at times, but we just didn't have the time or the money to be all that altruistic."

"I know, I know," she says with her "soft" voice. Most of the time her "regular" voice is businesslike, controlled. But her "soft" voice is what I love. It reminds me of her teen-age years, when she'd be singing to her (and my) heart's content. She had such a lovely, sweet voice. Bobby Vinton was her favorite then. I can still hear her singing *Blue on Blue*.

"I wish you'd sing more," I say, quite without obvious reason—at least to her. I loved it when she sang, "I believe for every drop of rain that falls . . . " I always wanted to take her in my arms and hug her then. Sometimes, when I did, she'd give a shy, almost embarrassed little smile, wriggle herself free, and say, "Now, don't let's get mushy, Mom."

"What?!" she says, in puzzled surprise. Then she giggles, "You're weird, Mother." We chat for a few more moments and part on a light-hearted note.

I remember, though, that incident with Greg almost made Bob and me irritated at her. "Let *her* take care of Greg," Bob had grumbled. "We've got enough on our hands."

Nevertheless, Greg did end up with us.

Neither one of us was too happy about the fact that once again we had a stranger in our house, with all the dependency on and need for us.

He had all sorts of problems that had to be taken care of first. The first one was his health; he had to have minor surgery before we could let him into our home—that meant to fight the battle with bureaucracy: getting welfare authorized, getting a medical assistance card, food stamps, doctor visits—a whole list of time-consuming tasks. Bob was at work, so I had to do all this, and it involved not only a lot of time, but some expenses for us and quite a bit of driving.

Finally, all that had been done, and he was happy to be with us.

He was a lanky, tall, handsome, and affectionate youngster with an unhappy childhood. He was also an epileptic, and that meant many doctor visits to be sure the medication was adjusted properly. Although he had to go to AA meetings (ordered by some agency), Bob and I weren't sure whether he was an alcoholic, but we took him to the meetings.

In time, he had found a part-time job, and I drove him there every morning and picked him up again. Since he worked in a delicatessen and bakery store, there were some reduced-price or free items now and then, and it always made him happy to be able to bring us something.

Eventually, I helped him get his driver's license (he could drive a car, though I never found out how he had learned without a learner's permit!). Now and then Bob let him use the car. He was quite dependable and always home on time—until that one evening.

I had noticed that he had been quite anxious during the whole day. I knew the reason; he was facing his court trial the following morning. It was obvious he was frightened.

We had gone to see the defense attorney authorized by the state to handle his case, and I thought that that would somehow reduce Greg's tension.

But that evening, when he had to go to his AA meeting, he was still tense. Bob and I held our breath, but placed faith in Greg's common sense and let him use the car.

When it became past the time he should have been home, we knew that trouble lay ahead.

It turned out to be a traumatic time.

When Greg wasn't home with the car at 2:00 in the morning, Bob called the police, and we were advised to report the incident as "unauthorized use of the car." We were not only worried about Greg's safety, but, should he be in an accident, about being sued.

Finally, at four in the morning, we heard a car drive onto the parking pad in front of the house. We looked and saw Greg crumpled up on the front seat. As we opened the car door, we were hit by an overpowering smell of alcohol.

The evening ended up with what seemed like a scene from a bad movie: Greg shouting and yelling, pulling up his sleeve to show us needle marks, stating defiantly that he had injected dope, going into the kitchen and coming back with a large kitchen knife, waving it threateningly around, and finally showing us some blood trickling down from his waist.

I took the knife away from him, looked at the wound (it was a minor cut), and fixed it with a Band-Aid® after cleaning it, although I felt more like grabbing him by the pants and throwing him out.

The next morning we went to court.

He had to go to jail until there would be a place for him in a drug rehabilitation center. For a few days I visited him there, then Bob and I took him to a drug rehabilitation center an hour-and-a-half away by car in an adjoining state.

We had told him that he had better make it—should he decide to run away, our door would be closed. He had a chance to make something of his life—he'd better use it.

For about three months all went well.

Bob and I made several trips to the center, always with some items, either homemade food (in bulk—everyone there had to share with the others) or something bought that he needed or some special little item for encouragement. Bob and I felt that as long as he was there we needed to be his family and be supportive.

Then one day a phone call came from the center telling us that he had run away.

I expected a phone call from Greg—and it came. He needed to pick up some of his things left at our house.

I told him I'd leave them outside near the mailbox, that I wouldn't be home. When I returned, his things were gone.

A few weeks later there was a phone call from Greg telling me he was somewhere in Virginia, that he had a job and a nice girl friend, that he was fine, and so on. I listened with a mixture of gratitude (I wanted to believe that it was all true) and doubts.

A few months later a phone call came from Florida, telling me much of the same.

Naturally, there was sadness within me; I wanted so much for him to be happy and lead a good life.

But I also knew that Bob and I had done what needed to be done; we had given another human being the chance to get back up on his feet. It was up to him to do it.

Now, thinking back to all this, I want to evaluate my feelings concerning it all: Did I have regrets? After all, Bob and I could have led a much more undisturbed, peaceful life without all these involvements.

I answer myself with a clear no.

Bob and I did what we felt we had to do. We didn't go out looking for involvements of that kind, but when placed on our doorstep, we couldn't just turn away.

Somewhere within me the phrase "Love thy neighbor as thyself" lingers.

15

That Something Still . . .

Today one of my friends celebrates her one-hundreth birthday. The invitation to celebrate places my emotions in turmoil: one hundred years—compared to Bob's sixty-five. Of course, I'm happy for my friend. She is a sweet, lovable, loving lady with a sound mind and that particular beauty of years spent well and happy. I feel privileged to be her friend.

But I also wish that Bob's life could have lasted one hundred years.

Tonight, I dread the evening walk for some reason. I try to put aside my feelings of depression, but it seems an impossible task. I end up crying, and I don't want to be alone.

I call my son Ron.

When he hears me crying on the telephone, he says, without waiting for an explanation, "Mom, I'll be right there. I'll spend the night. Don't you worry."

Within half an hour he is there. He hugs me, and I know he's trying hard not to cry himself.

Looking at him now, so grown-up and yet still vulnerable, my heart goes out to him in waves of tenderness. Oh, my children. I'm blessed with so much. How ungrateful of me to be sad!

Ron lies down on the couch watching TV trying to go to sleep, while I'm in my bedroom trying to do the same.

My son's presence has revived other memories—those of times before Bob came into the picture.

There is little twelve-year-old Ronnie, proud as can be because he just changed a flat tire on my car. Mama's little helper. Good-natured to a fault. He was so easily comforted. If he wanted something and I told him, "Perhaps tomorrow," he would say, "Okay," and that would be it. Quite in contrast to his sister, who would insist on having everything right there and then. Gloria, the pretty little "China doll," always neat and tidy, even when playing in mud that would leave other children completely dirty, was also very insistent on having her own way. Gloria, my little girl, who tried to cover up her vulnerability by being stubborn and then one day had to let down her guard when she had inadvertently closed the door on her pet, a talking parakeet, while he was sitting on top of the open door, crushing him. For a while I thought my darling would need to see a therapist, she grieved so much. And her attempts at cooking—she was good at that, too. I worked at the Johns Hopkins Hospital; I loved my job. Life was not easy, but I tried to make it easier. We did find time to go to the zoo, go to Washington, go swimming. But the marriage was not working. I couldn't protect them from the upset of a broken marriage, ending in separation and finally divorce.

All of us survived it.

I'm thinking about Ron and his moments of torture when his marriage ended. Perhaps it makes no difference whether a loss is produced by the death of a body or by the death of a love.

The day his wife left to return to California, Bob and I had visited Ron in his house. I had brought a meal along, but none of us had any appetite. Ron sat at the table, his eyes red from crying before we arrived there.

"You know," he said, half laughing, half crying, "life is so funny; I was trying to get something from the refrigerator before you got here. And all I could think of was 'shak'n bake,' 'shak'n bake.' Kathi must have explained to me that to fry chicken you use Shak'n Bake.® That phrase went through my head continually. Life is stupid, isn't it?" he said with a tormented smile.

I wanted to comfort him, my heart was filled with tears and pain for him. But he was never one for trite generalities. What should I have said? That life goes on? All wounds heal in time? There'll be something good around the corner sooner or later? And so I just hugged him. And Bob started telling us some funny incident from work, as a diversion.

Now here is my son, trying to comfort me. Knowing that his presence, as ours so long ago, would help ease the pain.

As I'm thinking about easing pain, I have to remember again the first Christmas without Bob.

The kind of gifts I received was overwhelming; almost everything had been selected with a special meaning relating to the circumstances in mind.

There was a lovely porcelain music box from Marcie, who always proclaimed herself our "adopted" daughter. For a number of years Bob and I had rented out one area of our house—Marcie had been one of those renters. Whenever there were troubles in her life, she came over to share her problems with us. One day, during an especially upsetting incident that happened to her in a mismatched love relationship, she said smiling from under her tears, "I come to you as though you were my parents. I might as well adopt you; from now on you're also my parents."

When Bob died, she was in shock, in pain.

Somehow, Bob must have known of this, because on her birthday, for which I had given her a framed photo of Bob and some other little items, she received a birthday present from someone whom she had known for quite some time but didn't like all that much, thinking that it was mutual. She was totally surprised by the gesture itself, but when she realized that the gift was a bouquet of violets, she almost fainted. I had told her about Bob's message for Margaret.

It's strange, but that year violets seemed to pop up from everywhere; I received cards with violets on them from people who knew nothing about communication with Bob, let alone messages from him. Wrapping paper, for some reason or other, had the violets theme on them. I came across miniature violets as I had never seen them before (reminiscent of the violets that grow on Circle Road). Violets had never grown on our lawn before; now they popped up everywhere.

I'm looking at a beautiful music box from Marcie; it's a pair of swans, a male and a female; he has his wings gracefully, protectively covering the female in a touching pose. I haven't been able to identify the tune. But I play it often; I've heard it before, but can't remember the name. "It reminds me of Mr. Chesney and you," Marcie smiled shyly as she handed me the present. It's precious to me.

John had given me a book that dealt with a study of the phoenix, all the way back into history. I read it the same day that the phoenix bola tie slid down from its nail to the poem.

From everywhere Bob seemed to touch me, even through the hands of friends, of people who loved me. I recognized every single gift as one of special importance and cherished it.

Knowing that my son is nearby in the other room, I have memories of another kind that weave their way through my mind, like a tapestry with irregular patterns of colors and shapes.

There was the day in court.

I had been working on two jobs to support my children and me—child support, little as it was, came only occasionally at first and then not at all. Then came the day of deception. The children's father had told me that it would be in their best interests if they could spend summer vacation with him on his friend's farm. I didn't like the idea of being without the children for such a long time, but was trying to be "sensible." My long working hours made it impossible to spend much time with them. It seemed only fair to let them have time with adults and perhaps some pets, warm sunshine, freshly picked fruits, and other little diversions from life in suburbia. And I could always visit them. The children's father promised to give me their address the day after he picked them up.

It was a great deception: I never received the address. My telephone calls to the company where he worked were left unreturned, always with the excuse that he "was not in." After days of exhausting tries, I finally took matters into my own hands. I had a general idea of the farm's location and on a Saturday, free from the job, I went about my search. I had taken the separation agreement, which stated clearly that the children were in my custody, and went to the state police office to plead for their help in finding them. At that time I found out that a separation agreement was worth next to nothing; I would have to get a court order. Still the kind heart of one of the officers could not ignore my despair, and he helped (unofficially, as he said) to guide me toward the location.

When the children saw me, I expected a sign of joy.

Instead, they looked at me with an expression on their faces I could not quite identify: surprised shock, somewhat guilty, somewhat ashamed, somewhat embarrassed. At first I was in shock over this reaction, then it dawned on me: they knew! They were part of this conspiracy! But how? How was this possible? Then the pieces fell together, the pattern of mind-poisoning that had begun some time ago: his day of picking them up for a visit with him and upon their return having two very rebellious, resentful, and disobedient children made it quite clear that something was being done to their image of me. While at first it was a puzzlement to me, now I saw clearly what had taken place.

I knew I would have to go to court. I had tried to avoid this to protect the children from the trauma of court proceedings, but now I had no choice.

The day had come—which I call "the day of infamy."

The children avoided my eyes.

When the judge asked them with whom they wanted to live, they stated that they wanted to live with their father.

"Naturally," I thought bitterly, "naturally, I'm the one who says, 'Do your homework, clean your shoes, help me with the dishes, tidy up your room,' and then say, 'We can't afford this,' not mentioning that perhaps with child support being paid as ordered, I would be able to afford a bit more."

It was a day I fought one of the hardest battles of my life within me: I fought to retain my faith in justice.

With obvious sympathy the judge told me that since the children had clearly stated so, he had no choice but to award custody to the father.

In a last attempt at gaining justice, I held up something my son had made for me for Mother's Day the previous year. It was a big heart, wrapped in silver foil, with a poem he had written on it:

> "Mother, you're so good to me
> You make me always want to be
> Kind to others all day long,
> You give my heart a happy song;

You are so good, so dear, so true:
I wish I could be just like you . . . "

I held this silver-foiled, dear, imperfect heart in front of the judge: "Does this look like something from children who don't love their mother?" The heart in my hand trembled—but not as much as the heart within me. In fact, I had a hard time stopping my heart from breaking into little pieces.

Of course, it didn't. Hearts are made of a strange mixture, all in accordance with requirements of the moment: softness of feather, steel and iron, resiliency and flexibility, wisdom and folly, tenderness and restraint, hope and despair, and fractions and fractions of all emotions possible. The heart is the assembly of the sum total of all being.

The judge looked away. "I'm so sorry," he said gently (and I knew he meant it), "but the children clearly stated." And I knew this was one day where he wished to have a profession other than that of a judge.

The children walked away with their father, still trying very hard to avoid looking at me. I talked to a lady from the Social Services agency who assured me that the children, given some time, would return to me, but I would have to do exactly as the agency suggested. She gave me comfort and advice, which I followed to the letter, and a few months later my daughter asked if she could come live with me again, and a few months after that my son followed suit.

I asked him, before I picked him up to bring him home to me, if he knew that there were household rules to live by and whether he would be willing to abide by them. His answer made me swallow hard. "Mom," he said, "at first I thought it was wonderful to be able to be out till 1:00 or 3:00 in the morning. I'm grown-up, I can stay out late, no questions asked—what a wonderful life! Then it dawned on me; they let me stay out without questioning because they didn't *care*."

I knew then that we would have a good and healthy family unit, Bob and the children and I. But I would have liked for my son to have his growing-up lesson at the age of thirteen in a gentler way.

Now he is trying so hard to be my comfort, my help, my strength. I'm grateful.

Nothing much happened on our evening walk tonight, nothing important had been said—Bob must have sensed that I was not in any shape to take in important subjects. He just reassured me of the afterlife as a reality.

Before falling asleep and aware of my son's protective presence in the other room, I reflect upon my blessings.

Perhaps—no, quite truly—I have been more fortunate than many other people in a similar situation. My family is as supportive as is possible for them; none of my friends has deserted me, but instead pay even more attention to me than ever before. They invite me to their homes. They call me on the telephone; they send me cards, books to read, send quotes relating in a positive way to matters concerning life and death; they shower me with their love. Underneath their loving support I can sense their own grief—they, too, loved Bob and miss him. From everywhere around me comes caring support. Surrounded with all these gifts, I have little time for destructive grief. I am able to continue living.

People tell me—in disbelieving surprise—that I look well. They all expected the opposite, of course. Everyone knew of the close relationship between Bob and me. Can I tell them my secret—that Bob *isn't* dead? That we talk to each other every evening? That I now *know* there is life after death?

I can tell some, but not all of them the details of my hope, of my own spiritual resurrection. I'm living proof to some people that there must be something very special that we, the human beings, are missing out on because though we *say* we believe in "life everlasting"—in reality we *don't*. We want our proof, our visible evidence, our scientifically proven formulas. We torture ourselves with doubt, when it's all so easy. We don't recognize the marvelous gift of "life forever," as God promised us, as it is written.

It no longer matters to me whether anyone believes that what I experience is real. It's no longer important; the sun hiding behind clouds is still the sun in existence, though hidden from view. In the concept of evolution a human's brain is that of a child. What do we know of space, of dimensions, of creation, of the universe, of time? Only what our brain, like a computer, is *conditioned* to accept in accordance with development.

But time—time is the clue to that which we don't know. If we could solve the mystery of time, we could solve all other unknowns. Time—like a string of pearls—glides through our fingers, one by one, then in a wave of mysterious imbalance (or balance?) connects itself again as a whole, as though it had never been any other way, making us wonder what is real and what is not. The cycle of eternity, of infinity: what do we know of it?

With frantic need the human existence compels humanity to eternally hunt for that elusive, precious, hard-to-hold item: happiness. And when we've found it, do we know what to do with it? Perhaps some of us do—at times.

> "O happiness! Our being's end and aim!
> Good, pleasure, ease, content! whate'er thy name
> That something still which prompts the eternal sigh,
> For which we bear to live, or dare to die ... "
> —Alexander Pope

I'm looking forward to tomorrow. Tomorrow Aline and Frances are coming for a visit to hear the rest of the tape.

I'm ready.

16

The Measure of Love

"But now abideth faith, hope, love, these three,
And the greatest of these is love."
—I Corinthians 13:13

F rances, Aline, and I are comfortably seated in the "big room," coffee and tea at our fingertips. It's evening, and the room radiates an atmosphere of warmth.

The other side of the tape starts with Carl and me saying something that I can't identify, but it's only a short sentence. Then I hear Carl say something like " . . . and he put his hand on your head . . . " with me continuing, "and I looked right into his eyes . . . " Pause. Then, I say, "You know something? All my life . . . maybe *all* lifetimes . . . hah, it's funny; I'm just recognizing it . . . I never forgot those eyes. Something in them . . . it's not definable. I cannot put it into words. And I was always looking for eyes like that. For the quality that would radiate from them, you know. And the closest I have come ... on that ... was my husband." Pause. Then, "My God, I didn't recognize that ... but I can see the eyes ... " Pause. Then, in a whisper of awe: "My God ... I could draw them ... " Long pause.

Carl: "What are these eyes saying to you now?"

"Same thing they said then." My voice is quite composed and natural, my everyday voice. "What you have to picture is ... " It's obvious that I'm searching for adequate words to describe the eyes of Jesus and am struggling to do so. " ... a total collection of all the good things, all the good feelings in life. Combined. In other words: if you can picture love and forgiveness and kindness, compassion, and put them all into a definite kind of color ... or whatever ... there was just something ... It's incredible that it *can* be in ... " I interrupt myself, very matter-of-fact: "You know, it's funny, I'm just recognizing something else; I've always looked in people's eyes. I can see or feel something ... " Pause. "I must have been looking for a long, long time ... " Long pause.

After a period of silence, Carl picks up again: "I wonder if you'll recall perhaps the first time there when you heard of this man. What's turned your awareness to his existence?"

My answer comes very quickly. "On the mountain." It's definite in its nuance. "So that must not have been the first time I was there. I didn't feel like I was a stranger there, anyway. But I think there was nothing behind me. In other words, when I saw the 'Massada' incident ... that was like there were caves or something there. There wasn't anything there, just a platform. So I must have walked around the mountain, for whatever purpose. I think I wanted to be alone. I could meditate there or whatever. It was a nice, quiet spot, and I always liked a big view, you know ... Now, what I'd like to know and find out for myself is ... how did I find out on that mountain ... "

"Yes ... " Carl supports.

"The first name that comes to mind is ... hah," I give a

slight chuckle of disbelief, "is—of all names—Margaret . . . But, I don't know." I seem to disbelieve my own words. "I'm not sure . . . " Pause. "I must have been pretty young. We were playing something . . . something like . . . marbles? Of course, they didn't have marbles in those days. We played with some rolling things—whatever they were. And I don't remember what the game was . . . but it was a little bit like marbles. Maybe it's as old as that—I don't know." I seem to be laughing at myself. "Just little stones . . . Maybe that's what I had in my pouch."

"Did you play this game with someone else there?"

"Yeah." That comes very sure. "I don't know whether it's Martha or Margaret. I'm not sure. And . . . " Pause. Then a surprised: "Hmm . . . I'm trying to picture how she's dressed." I cannot determine at this point, listening to the tape, what it is that seemed to have caused that surprised "hmm." "She's dressed pretty much the same way I am. And her hair is long, she wears a different kind of belt. And she's barefoot. I have like a . . . like a golden belt. She's got like a leather belt or something like that on, or cloth—I'm not sure. But it isn't a tie-belt—it's got something, I don't know what. Anyway, we're playing . . . and she was very enthusiastic, I think she had heard him. And she said I should go with her and see him. And I think we had to, somehow, come up with an excuse. We weren't really allowed to go that far. We were pretty far away." Pause. " 'Cause, he was all over the place, that's the thing, you know, and I mean, you either had to be a 'camp follower,' as they say, or you had to be lucky and be at the spot where he was just appearing." Pause. "So, when we went to see him, we had to make quite a walk, almost a day trip. And we had to take some water and things with us . . . although I think we could have picked up water anywhere. It wasn't like we had to go across the desert or anything like that. Or maybe I picture it longer than it was. Or maybe the wait was so long, I don't know."

"And in a child's mind . . . " Carl ventures.

"Yeah." Pause. "As a matter of fact, maybe I was about twelve years old. Twelve, or thirteen, or fourteen..." Pause. "Maybe younger; maybe ten or so. Doesn't matter." Pause. Time of long silence.

"Now, what's coming to you?" Carl queries gently, softly.

"It...there is an enclosure, with wood beams, you know, like a fence...but the wood put into wood..." I describe some more of this "enclosure." "And we have to get across that. To get to where we have to go. He's not in there—we've just got to get across that. It's kind of 'icky'—they may have been keeping some animals in there, maybe like a cow-pen or something. Or an animal-pen or whatever, but it's kind of 'icky,' and we're barefoot. This time I'm barefoot, too. And then we climb it, and we go across...now, I don't know why I'm seeing a meadow. Not very thick, but some kind of green meadow. And I don't think they *had* meadows there. But they must have, let's face it; they had to eat or feed some animals, too. And...it's a little bit hilly...and...oh, boy! It's nighttime! Evening, rather, and we're supposed to be home." Pause. "But we just wanted to stay." Pause. "I didn't understand much of what he said that time. It was two years later when I saw him again." Pause. "I try to remember what he said...at least a little bit..."

After a short silence, my voice continues, "Oh, I think I know why I didn't understand; he was talking about Pharisees—and that didn't...you know, hit home with me that time..." Pause.

"How did he impress you?" Carl asks.

"Very strongly. But I was a bit in awe. I don't think I fully understood what he was all about then. But you know, it must have sunk in, and—of course—along those two years I must have heard things that reinforced or changed that feeling of awe. I was a little bit frightened the first time." Pause.

"And you knew what it was like to be frightened?" Carl probes.

"I don't know . . . I wasn't terribly frightened, you know, it was just . . . "

"Awesome," Carl completes.

"Yeah. It was somehow strange, and besides, I think what added to the fact, that I was supposed to be home. You know, I was a little nervous." Pause. "My mother wasn't angry with me when I told her—except they were frightened." Pause. "She said she, too, had heard of Jesus." Pause. Long silence.

Then, "I know, up there, on the mountain, I really wanted to be with these people . . . " Long pause. "I think it's possible that . . . may . . . have been . . . the last time . . . that Jesus could heal . . . maybe that's why I got that overpowering feeling of sadness and pain. Because it's possible that the people who went to see him had an inkling . . . " Pause, and then, almost in a whisper of recognition: "I think they *knew* . . . That's why they were all dressed in black, or in dark clothes . . . my God, they *knew* . . . " Long silence.

Then, reflectively, quietly, "Strangely enough . . . 'cause, I didn't see anybody coming back . . . so if they came from behind the mountain there on this road and behind there was Jesus . . . " I'm debating with myself, trying to analyze the directions, and then: " . . . Jesus . . . but it wasn't there, it was to the right . . . it all came from over there . . . " Pause. Deep sigh.

Carl: "Now what's coming?"

"Oh, things want to come," my voice is casually rebellious, "but I don't want to. I'm tired."

"There was one particular memory," Carl changes the subject, "that you died with there . . . something I'm sure was in your mind . . . so what's the first thing that's coming to you . . . want you to connect in with that."

"I have to picture myself dying. That's hard to do, you know, switch back and forth. I have to put myself into it . . . " Pause. Long silence. "Well, I think this is just repeating a phrase I've heard: 'May God have mercy on my soul . . . ' "

Listening to this puzzles me: I'm too casual, too much attempted avoidance there. "But I wouldn't say that. Me, now. I don't believe in saying things like that... although... I believe in God having mercy on someone's soul. But then again, I feel we are responsible for our own soul development, and in God's kindness and mercy... we don't have to ask Him for it."

"That was a long time ago," Carl says.

"Yes." That comes precise and clearly.

"A long time ago," Carl repeats.

Long silence. Carl says nothing for a while to prompt a response. Then he whispers, as though he has picked up something within my psyche, "All right, what's coming?"

"For a while there... " my voice is a painful whisper, "it's so... " I'm softly crying, " ... so... demeaning... but it isn't ... it's not like me... but I *did*... " My crying is now more pronounced, "On my hands... and knees crawl along the cross... but then I thought that didn't help much... and I got up and I walked away for a little bit... " The pain in my voice affects me even now. "I want to get away from there." I say it almost with angry, defiant annoyance.

"That hurt, didn't it?" Carl says.

The "yes" from me is a whisper. "I want to get away from there!" That comes with determination.

"You recall the fondest time, your favorite teaching," Carl tried to divert with his gentle, deep voice.

"Okay... let's see... " trying to regain composure. "I try to capture his presence. That's the only way I can get the feeling, it's the only way I remember the words... " The emotional drain shows in my voice. Pause. "He said that one of the harder things to do—all of the things he taught were hard to do in many ways—because to be unselfish is difficult when it means sacrificing, but he doesn't really *want* sacrifice. He didn't believe in sacrifice. He believed in ... giving because of *love*. And willingly. And that... it does not mean anything if you do something that you don't do with your full heart, because God is in everybody's heart and soul, and you can't really fool God. So pretending isn't going to do anything. It's got to be real, and that's the hardest part because the foundation for it all is love. So, if we could just learn to love properly and unselfishly, then that would be the answer to all the problems."

Pause. Then it continues: "I always kind of fought that issue a little bit. I questioned it then, because I don't think love alone is enough. And he got very upset with me. He said that I was not old enough to know what love could do. And the miracle love could perform. And that if I would have doubts about that, I'd better forget ever thinking that I could love . . . Not the kind of love . . . in other words, what Jesus was talking about was the love of humankind . . . love in general, not different kinds of love. Just love. The feeling of love, the concept of love."

"And you had a taste of that love," Carl says gently.

A firm "yes." After a short pause, "I had a taste of it then, and I had a taste of it in this lifetime . . . and I do know its strength. And I do know now that Jesus was right. Maybe it took me all these lifetimes to figure it out . . . " Pause. Then, with a small laugh, "But I . . . would you believe? I hear myself still say, 'Love alone is not enough' . . . I can't believe it!" Carl is laughing along with me. "I'm too practical and realistic about it." I end my laughter by saying, "But the thing is, you see, Jesus knew the total concept of love. I don't. But I get an inkling—and he is right, of course. But to apply it, one would have to be Jesus. But I can't be Jesus . . . I can't be half as . . . "

"That's all right," Carl says, to get us off the subject. "That's something you'll have to struggle with, learn over . . . "

"Oh, I don't even want to be," I laugh again, interrupting him.

After that, Carl begins to count to bring me out of hypnosis.

Fully conscious again and after exchanging a few more

words, I had left Carl and driven home.

Aline and Frances have sat silent throughout the tape-playing. It's strange how it exhausts me just listening to the tape. All of this puzzles me. Had I really had a "past-life memory"? Or is there something hidden in my subconscious that needs to come out? I voice my quandary to my two friends—I know they'll be totally honest with me. And they are certainly well-educated, intelligent people with their feet on the ground.

Both Frances and Aline believe it was real, as did Carl, the hypnotherapist. Why can't I fully believe it? Why am I such a doubter?

I am not a religious fanatic, but perhaps there is more spiritual sense in me than I ever suspected.

I had known from childhood that thoughts can overcome barriers of time and space. God fitted into my concept of the total scheme of things in perfect unison with the universe, with life, with love, with existence, as the totally supreme, loving, caring Being. When some could not find any reason for living other than biological, I knew instinctively that there was more to life than met the eye. What was it that was more to life than that? Weren't we, the human beings, just a tiny speck, a dot, in our existence in comparison to the universe? Yes, we *were* that, but we were also blessed with a thinking brain and a feeling soul. "Created in His image," it says in the Bible. Also, small as the atom and other related objects are, they are still extremely powerful. So what was, what *is*, our purpose? But who says that there has to be a purpose? Isn't it enough that we *do* exist?

If the tape is a "past-life memory," then there must be a reason for my memory having been revived. Not necessarily so, my mind tells me. Why should there be a reason for this, when memory is either there or is not? One hardly asks why one remembers events from everyday living in this particular, conscious lifetime. The only difference between that and a past-life memory is a time factor and with it a trans-

formation of life forms—temporarily. If one would look at
the concept, taught to us, of "life everlasting," then we may
consider that it does *not* state "*one* life everlasting" and
could, therefore, indicate that it is merely a matter of perception. How far can we see? Only as far as our eyesight permits.

But something else is working in my subconscious. It has
to do with Jesus. The tape has revealed something I didn't
know before, a connection I never knew existed. What is it
that lingers within the confines of my mind, prompting and
probing, like a question unanswered?

"Question unanswered." That's it! Within a second the
past-life regression session, which took place about six
years ago, flares up in my memory like a shooting star. Bob
had explained to me that evening what he understood from
the Edgar Cayce readings, about the general concept of
more than one life. After he had gone to sleep, I pondered
over the question whether and how Jesus fit into this concept.

Now I *know*.

The key phrase is "*I am the way*."

But now I also know what "I am the way" means.

Jesus came to us in the form of our own human existence
so that we could *see* the miracle of faith, of belief. Trying to
overcome flaws and inequities, humankind can survive. If
"love thy neighbor as thyself" is as important as Jesus said
and if we learn to live by that rule, then each individual will
have reached an extremely high level of development, ad-
vancing at a rapid speed toward completion of a life cycle—
regardless of how many times an existence in a body or
other life form—with the purpose of redoing the origin:
God. Jesus was the living, visible proof that it can be done.
Perhaps that is the purest form of resurrection.

I share these thoughts with Aline and Frances.

"Remember," Frances says, "you once told me about a
book you read. I think it was called *What Dreams May Come*.

You said one sentence in it had impressed you very much: 'We're not punished or rewarded *for* our deeds, but *by* them.'"

"In other words, 'cause and effect,' " Aline says.

"Somehow like planting a seed, the seed of a rose cannot turn into a mulberry bush," I add. "It's the same with seeds of love, isn't it?"

"Right," Aline nods. "And to go further: If humankind could see the total picture, it would be easier to comprehend what's at stake with preserving the environment. To quote a saying from the Bible: 'The Lord by wisdom has founded the earth, by understanding has he established the heavens.' " (Proverbs 3:19)

"You mean that it's our duty to preserve the environment, since it's also God's creation, and that this is also part of 'love thy neighbor'?"

"Well," Aline smiles, "I didn't mean it quite that way—but you have a point there. The earth is our habitat; it would be difficult, I believe, to find something equally beautiful, don't you think?"

"What about the last part? The part about 'understanding'?"

"I'm not sure myself. But I think it means that God knows us and understands that we need more than the physical realm. Anyhow, it's late. I think I'd better go home now."

My two friends leave, but I don't feel alone.

Somehow I know there'll be a lot more to come. But for now I'm tired.

17

The Spring of All My Joy

"This is the generation of him that seek him, that seek Thy face . . . "
—Psalm 24:6

Naturally I'm no exception from anyone else; someone close to you dies, and you wonder if you did something you shouldn't have or were remiss in doing something you should have done.

Do I have regrets? Could I have saved Bob's life? No. The attendants who came with the ambulance told me later on that even if Bob had been in the hospital when the heart attack took place, he would have died. The attack was just too massive. Should I have been more persistent in making him have his checkups? That's questionable. People have told me that someone they loved had died a day after a thorough checkup. Did I do everything in my power to make

Bob happy? Yes—just as much as he tried to make me happy. Did he try too hard to do that and with that used up his energies, attempting my altruistic endeavors? I don't think so. I knew him well enough to know that a firm "no" of protest could be expected when Bob felt it was too much. He was a good man—a man filled with compassion and understanding, but he was not weak—he knew when to say no.

I remember the time period when I had decided to go back to work to help with the income. At first he protested, but I convinced him that while we had enough to live on, there was no money for a little pleasure. And it would be nice to be able to put a little money aside. For emergencies and old age.

Reluctantly he agreed that perhaps it wasn't a bad idea after all.

I found a job in one of the local mental hospitals as "Nursing Personnel Liaison" (a fancy title, for the position was building secretary!) and enjoyed the work tremendously. The job was a challenge. Three people before me had quit within an eight-month time period. Everyone in charge was new at the job, and an adequate system had not yet been established. But I liked it; I had a lot of contact with the patients, who were troubled teen-agers. They came to me for a little unprofessional, but loving TLC.

After I had worked there for a number of months, I had become quite familiar not only with the patients, but with the occasional upheavals.

Once again there had been an uproar at the building. It was difficult to determine what had caused it. But one of the patients had gone berserk and was fighting off two attendants who were trying their best to hold him down and calm him. He fought like a wildcat.

Alerted by the commotion outside in the hall, I walked out of my office toward him and started talking to him, trying to hug him, hoping to calm him down the way you would an infant in a temper tantrum. It worked. He started crying, and the attendants were able to escort him back to his room.

After work that day, with permission from the staff, I went to the hall and talked to all of the troubled youngsters.

"Listen," I said, "I have an idea. If all of you, the whole hall, will behave for two weeks—no smuggled alcohol or drugs, no incidents, no sassing back to the staff, and other little annoyances—if you really try to be good, then I'll try to get permission for all of you to come to my house for a party. We'll have hamburgers and hot dogs. I'll bake a strawberry torte with whipped cream. And we'll make a campfire outside on the lawn and roast marshmallows. But no alcohol or drugs—you know that I enjoy my life in full control of my senses."

"Oh, Inga! You *really* would do that? Have us over to your house?" They were disbelieving. And then, "Oh, they won't let us."

"Well, we shall see. Do what I suggested. In the meantime I'll try to get permission."

For the next two weeks I saw nothing but little angels with halos walking around the halls!

The door to the hall had been unlocked, and not one incidence of disturbance had occurred.

The day I had made my promise to them, on the way home, I reflected upon this. I wasn't looking forward to telling Bob about my impulsive action; he would certainly put up a good fight. He was a kind man, but he liked his comfort and peace. And I couldn't blame him. My own two children had been enough of a challenge! In turn, of course, they loved him, but rearing children is never easy.

Was I foolish in having made such a promise?

I remembered the picture of John, when we had visited him on his birthday. He had unwrapped his presents, and it was hard to tell whether he was enjoying them or not. He had thanked us, but I was a bit disappointed in his reaction.

Still, that's typical for most youngsters his age, with his emotional make-up. To show any sign of emotion was a "no-no." He had wanted one of those Western-style hats, the fashion of that day among his peer group. He looked very handsome in it when he tried it on. His long, harvest-blond, wavy hair, his beard and mustache, reminded me of someone: Christ. Was that intentional? Was there a hidden longing for something? Often, when I looked at these youngsters—troubled, lonely, searching for something, hungry for some unknown item to add depth or meaning to their lives, all in their lookalike, bearded, long-haired appearance—I wondered if subconsciously it displayed the longing for a need to find their higher self, their real inner self. Was that, perhaps, the reason for their involvement with drugs? If reality is without a challenge, without the exhilaration of being lifted out of the daily unexciting routine to a higher level of feeling, of soul development—is there, then, a type of ecstasy through drugs that does that, that lifts them up to realms they can otherwise not reach? Should organized religion not be able to do that? What is it that is lacking in our churches that turns our youth away into exploring other ways of reaching spiritual exaltation? Is it, perhaps, a lack of sincerity in our routine of worship they can sense and reject? Have we become spiritual robots? Or have we, the older generation, simply failed in our task of rearing our children with the right attitude by making things too easy for them? Youth needs a challenge. Have we exercised and practiced the *right* kind of love?

I had not anticipated all these thoughts would enter my mind just because of my impulsive action. I had had my challenge during and after the war. When you dig deep to try to find gold, you may well find a nest full of monsters instead.

I had ended up, after the war, with my own answers; to keep my faith simple. The more I questioned, the more questions arose. But deep down inside of me something was smoldering: the hint of something more, something wonderful, something I once knew, but had lost in the process of living and was still wanting.

I had reached home, and now I had to tell Bob.

As I expected, he was not pleased.

"Inga," he said with stern discomfort, "do you realize what you're doing? You're going to have about twenty disturbed teen-agers in this house! If they weren't disturbed, they wouldn't be where they are! It's bad enough to be surrounded by so many teen-agers, but from a *mental hospital* to boot! Boy, oh, boy, you're asking for trouble!"

"No, I'm *not!*" I defied his opinion. "They're wonderful youngsters. Besides, they'll have a staff member with them, you know."

"One against twenty," he grumbled. "But have it your way. No matter what I'd say, you'd win anyway."

But then, when the day of the party came and he was helping me with the preparations, he seemed to enjoy it, too.

The bus came and, in happy disarray, threw out a bundle of laughing and excited young humanity.

"Oh, Inga, what a beautiful place! I love it! It's so warm, so cozy! Oh, look at the back yard! Look! Is that where the raccoons come at night? Are they going to come tonight, too?" Their happy exuberance transmitted itself to Bob and me while we were trying to get them to settle down.

"Boy! Does that smell good! Can I have two pieces of the strawberry tor . . . tor . . . what do you call it?"

"Torte," I laughed. "And, yes, you may have two. There's plenty."

After they had eaten, we sat outside for a while. The sun was setting, it was getting dark. A warm breeze gently caressed the flushed faces, and some reflection from the evening sun placed patterns of varying design across their bodies, like a stage play of shadow images.

On my button accordion I was playing the few American

songs I knew: *Yellow Rose of Texas, The Green Green Grass of Home, Battle Hymn of the Republic,* and some others: a strange array of music for those youngsters used to rock and roll! I had cautiously played only one song at first, waiting for their reaction; I was afraid they might laugh! But they sat there with an expression on their faces that showed nothing but gentle, relaxed contentment, and when I played *Shenandoah,* they were singing along—shyly at first, then louder and with confidence.

Bob and I looked at each other, and we both knew each other's thoughts: *these* were the teen-agers who went to rock concerts and went wild and wacky?!

Suddenly it started raining—just a few drops, but we all ran inside. "Dammit! We wanted to roast marshmallows!" Their disappointment made them forget their language manners for a moment. Occasionally, in the hospital, I had heard them use stronger language, although they always tried not to use it in my presence.

"We can roast them inside, too," I consoled them. "Look at the bright side; maybe this way you'll see some raccoons."

A few minutes later a cheeky-looking, masked bandit peeked into the window.

"Hey. Look! Look! There's one!" Excitedly they all pushed against the window.

"Do you feed them, Inga?"

"Yes. Watch."

They're tame toward me. I can pet them, talk to them, they're well behaved and charming. Looking back into my living-room windows, I saw faces with wide-open eyes peek at me as I was petting the raccoons.

We roasted marshmallows on the open gas flame, and now we had the radio on with some of their kind of music.

Soon—too soon for them—it was time to leave.

I got about twenty-one hugs, some kisses. And a lot of loving feelings radiated toward me, and Bob had a very satisfied smile on his face. Within my heart I felt a mixture of joy and sadness: so much young hope, so much young pain. And so easily, at least for a few moments, smoothed over with a blanket of emotional velvet. I could not heal their pain forever or solve their problems, but I could, with an act of love, give a vision of things possible.

After the bus had left, as Bob and I were walking back into the house, Bob said lovingly, "Well done, honey, well done."

"Yes," I almost whispered it to myself, "but only because of you, because you love me, because you give me all I need."

I didn't know if he had heard me. But it didn't matter.

Love doesn't have to be audible—it can silently transmit its message.

As I'm reflecting upon the past, and in order not to let the pain of loss engulf me, I'm letting Bendahouse wrap me into the comfort of familiar sounds: the ticking of clocks; the refrigerator turning on and off; the air conditioner clicking when in service; the "pitter-patter" of little feet on the roof; the raccoons playing and chasing each other; a mockingbird belting out a love song—familiar sounds, familiar feelings—"but *love* is the greatest of them all."

Oh, *love!*

Curse and salvation—intertwining, blending, saving, destroying—pain and pleasure. *Where* lies the line of demarcation? Do only we humans feel the difference?

But without love, we would be robots.

And who wants to be a robot?

18

A Touch of Evil?

C hristmas is approaching.
Another one without Bob.
I dread it.

It seems as though the world outside—the *whole* world—pays not one ounce of attention to the pain within... Holding the burden of cold snow with serene dignity, the trees stand firm and detached from the human frailties that govern our attitudes. "Look at us," they seem to be saying, "we are here. And when the load gets too heavy, a branch may break off. So, what of it? Soon a new branch will appear somewhere from out of the trunk; from the sand-covered system of roots. So look at us; we're here. We live.

We do what is natural: survive."

Somehow my own inner voice no longer supports my needs. I cling with all my strength to the positive thought of the birth of Christ: birth, life, death, resurrection. And Bob had said, "Harmony is the balance of love—love of the law of the universe." I must remember everything Bob is telling me. I don't as yet fully understand all he's telling me. Some day in the future I probably will.

For right now, though, it looks as though I'm not even going to be here for Christmas but in Florida. Helen has called and told me that there's a contract on her house and would I please come. I don't want to go, I want to be here with my family and friends. But Helen has fallen and hurt her back, she tells me, and she can't walk, has to stay in bed.

Of course, I agree to see her and take care of the sale and all connected tasks: settlement, selling furniture, getting some pieces moved to my house here in Baltimore, taking Helen for doctor visits, getting a termite company to do their job, taking Helen to banks for transfer of funds and accounts, and all the other tasks of moving.

The flight had been smooth and quick. I had rented a car, and when I had arrived I had found a very grateful, but exhausted-looking Helen. I have to admit that the warm Florida sunshine feels good. And Helen's house was bright and cheerful, with a beautiful swimming pool outside the patio. Her husband Milton had died just a few years ago. She had, in my opinion, never outgrown the resulting depression.

Helen and I have just had dinner. She hasn't eaten very much, and soon she wants to go to sleep. I watch television for a few minutes, then I go to my room to read a book before going to sleep.

The guest room is small, but equipped with all necessities, even my own bath. When I had first entered it upon my arrival, it had struck me as very strange that one wall of the room was painted with dark arrows pointing downward from the ceiling. It had given me a very eerie feeling which didn't last very long—Helen's needs overpowered all else. "When we bought the house," Helen had explained, "we didn't like those horrible black arrows one bit. We planned to have the room painted or wallpapered, but since we hardly ever used the room, it was not a priority. And then Milton got sick and pondered over it, though. Why? Why would anyone want such an ugly wall? Someone had told us that two men had lived here and that there had been quite a few disturbing incidents of violence taking place here. But people would tell us just so much and no more. I must admit," she concluded with a resigned attitude, "after Milton died, I had to use quite a bit of willpower not to dwell on that story." She sighed, and we went on to other subjects. Now, with darkness outside, lying in my bed reading, I find I can't concentrate on the book.

The atmosphere in the house is one of depression, of gloom.

It's overwhelming, and I find it difficult to fight the urge to run. I remember Helen telling me, at the very beginning of my visit, that she had sensed this feeling that the house radiated at night for a long time. "Sometimes," she had said with a trace of fear left on her facial expression, "sometimes at night I thought I heard the sound of someone—or some-*thing*—walking past the foot end of my bed. It made a swishing sound—you know, like someone slowly dragging their feet, like a scuba diver with flippers. Everytime I heard it I got goosebumps." She had shivered at the memory of this. "I would hide my face under my pillow and pretend it didn't exist, that I was hallucinating. But then the next night it would happen again. Ah, I don't want to think about it." She cut herself short, trying to shake off the memory.

Now here I am, in this room with the black arrows. Has Helen's story influenced my thinking? Hardly, I answer myself, and with a tinge of bitterness: whoever has experienced the invasion of Berlin in 1945 and all its connected horrors has been "seasoned."

I go into the living room, trying to divert myself by watching television. The feeling of gloom, depression, and some kind of danger persists. It isn't a sense of being in *physical* danger, rather one of mental or emotional threat. It's something difficult to define. It has me puzzled and frightened at the same time. I have never before in my life experienced anything quite like it; I can face dangers presented to me by other people, but not this unknown, creeping, depleting, insidiously subtle attempt at invading my inner being, perhaps my soul.

Come on! I reproach myself, come on! You're just homesick! You're upset because it's Christmas and you're away from home. So get a grip on yourself!

It doesn't help. I go outside to the edge of the pool, hoping that its refreshing fragrance and a look at the beautiful stars and sky will remove the feeling of gloom and unknown fear.

I feel better outside, under the open sky.

After a while I get very tired and with apprehension reenter the living room.

Again, after a few minutes inside the room, I have the feeling I want to run—run away! But I know I can't leave Helen alone in here, in this house with two personalities: the cheerful, sunny one at daytime and the threateningly gloomy and frightening one at night.

I will conquer this, I tell myself again. It's ridiculous to let a feeling overpower me! I try to remember Helen's and my evening hours together. We had even laughed a bit before she went to bed. Somehow during our conversation I had laughingly said something about *fait accompli,* and now, just as a diversion, I try to translate it into English. Let's see now, *fait accompli.* Ah, yes, it would mean, "it is done."

As I hear this phrase in my mind, I am suddenly, in the flash of a second, transferred back in time. Two thousand years ago that was said by someone, someone special, someone dear to me, someone who had died. Had I heard it being said?

Oh, my God, that pain. It engulfs my soul and spirit, cuts through my heart in agonizing torment.

I start crying violently.

It only lasts a few minutes, then I'm quite calm again and feel as though a fresh breeze is gently sweeping through the house.

The feeling of depression, of gloom has left.

Suddenly I'm very tired. I go to bed, and before I have a chance to evaluate the events, I'm deep asleep.

With all the activities going on, involving the sale of the house, dissolving a whole household, the continuing doctor visits, planning the trip back to Baltimore with Helen, and all the other time-consuming little details, I have very little time left to think about the darker side of life. But then, finally, all is done, and Helen and I are in the airplane on our way.

I feel as though I've been released from prison—and that has nothing to do with the house or the situation itself, I know. No—what happened was something quite different; it was a touch from the dark side, a touch from the forces that we do not normally (at least not knowingly) deal with. The question, however, is *why*. Why did it happen when it did, and why did it take place at Helen's house, and why at Christmas time? Was I supposed to learn something from it? Was it a warning? A memory? All of the above?

Helen has fallen asleep next to me, and I have two hours in which to ponder over this. I'm not all certain that there'll ever be any answers to these questions. I'm sure of one thing, though. I neither imagined nor exaggerated the atmosphere existing in the house. During the war I experienced danger—lots of that. *Humanmade* danger, that is; and I knew how to deal with that. This was different; I knew I was exposed to forces beyond any experience I've ever had. The psychological contents of my mind were rational, and although I tried—in an attempt at avoiding the real issue—to talk myself into believing that my mind was perhaps overworked, that I needed more sleep, more rest, my gut feeling told me otherwise.

Helen had told me about the "swishing" footsteps past her bed; this was not something I could ever explain. I could only analyze my own experience, and there I had *some* thoughts. The tape of my hypnosis session (if that was not a manufactured figment of my imagination) indicated that I had apparently witnessed the crucifixion of Jesus.

During the few times I had played the tape to myself and listened to my voice relating incidents that my conscious mind would not allow to come forth, I was amazed at my emotional reaction. It was painful to even just *listen* to it. I had not been a regular churchgoer, I hardly ever talked about God or biblical themes, and though I prayed, I had not done so on a regular basis. During the past three decades of my life I had thought about Jesus only occasionally, mostly (as many Christians, I hate to admit) on special occasions like Christmas or Easter. However, when I was twelve years old and learned all about Christ, I had felt a very strong connection to and with this person, or spirit, called Jesus of Nazareth. It hadn't lasted more than perhaps two years, then life (especially war) took over. It appeared to me only one more time in strong force at the end of the war with all its traumatic effects. After that it was routine again.

Had I been "emotionally dead" during all these years, and Bob's death brought to the surface what had lain asleep? Hardly. Loving Bob, my children, his children, my family, my friends was certainly a very strong emotional force in my life. His death couldn't change that—especially in view of the events that took place after he died.

I was reasonably sure that the tape did not consist of fabrications of my mind. The emotional impact was just too strong.

Assuming, then, that the tape was a genuine past-life memory—why was I remembering now and not at some other time? Was that important? If I hadn't wanted to stop smoking and hadn't gone for hypnosis to Carl Schlotter-beck, the memory may never have entered my conscious mind. There was no reason to believe that there was any special meaning to either the place or time of its occurrence; it seemed to be just a memory revived—for whatever reason. Certainly, if I could remember, so could others.

The emotional impact of Bob's death opened a "channel," a receiving station for transmission, available to *all* of us. In the beginning, after it happened, my mind searched for explanations; I compared the human mind to a house with several locked doors, with some of us humans having one or more doors open than others, but all of us with the ability to open a few more doors to see what was beyond. My door had been slammed open by shock. Instead of being frightened by the unknown, I had explored it. I saw a dark room, but each step that I took to see more, the room illuminated itself, showing me its contents. Now I know more than I knew before.

The voice of the flight attendant disrupts my thoughts by announcing the need to fasten our seat belts; we're ready to land.

I can't wait to get home. Christmas was delayed this year; the family and I had agreed to celebrate the holy season on the twelfth day of Christmas.

The touch by the dark side is almost forgotten. But I *have* learned something—that evil can also be intangible. Until these moments in Florida I knew of evil, but it was far away, even though very concrete—recognizable in human form.

Was there any meaning to my experiences? Is there a reason why I felt I had made a connection with evil, especially in view of the fact that nothing really bad had happened? After all, it was just a sensation, a feeling. But perhaps therein lay the reality of the occurrence.

As always, my thoughts don't dwell on things I can't explain. I'm always hoping for answers—at some time.
For now I just want to go home.

19

A Helping Hand

"How dreadful knowledge of the truth can be,
When there's no help in truth!"
—Sophocles, *Oedipus Rex*

I had to make a big decision; in spite of the fact that I suspected Helen to be a drinking alcoholic, I had to offer her the opportunity to live with me. To come to that conclusion was difficult, and I had spent many nights pondering the pros and cons. Once before in my life I had been involved in helping with that disease, with success, but in Helen's case it might be another matter. She was close to seventy years old; it had been a way of life for her for many years.

Would I be able to handle the stress?

I would at least have to try it.

It meant one more visit to Florida, and it would be a

strenuous one. I had ten days in which to sell her house, dissolve her household, get her and some furnishings and personal belongings packed and ready to go.

Before her arrival here, I had to do a task I dreaded; I had to get a room ready for her. It was the room that Bob and I had used as an office or study. It contained stacks and stacks of Bob's notes: notes from college days, from his work in the oil fields as a geologist, correspondence, notes and remarks, excerpts from his and others' writings, old bills and check stubs, copies of architectural drawings and plans. In short, the room was filled with tons of paperwork.

Having to sort through all this was not only a hard physical task, but also a tremendous emotional strain. It was something I may have been ready to do years from now, but just yet I could not randomly throw away anything; I had to sort through all of it. Had it not been for my love for Helen, I could not have done it—the pain of loss hit me each time I touched one of his notes.

Once I almost had a breakdown; there were the samples of Bob's first attempt at automatic writing. I remembered well the day (not long ago, it seemed) when Bob had retreated into his "office" for quite some time, and when I hadn't heard from him for a while, I went in to see whether he was all right.

"Oh, honey," he disarmed my concern with his charming smile, "I'm just fine. Guess what I just did?" He showed me some unidentifiable scribbling that looked something like an electrocardiogram. "I tried some automatic writing. I don't know if I got anything—but it's a beginning."

Before I had a chance to take a look at it the phone rang and I had to run back into the living room. Then later on I forgot all about it. Apparently Bob did, too—the subject never came up again.

Three months later he was dead.

Then, in preparing Helen's room for her, as I was sorting through all the paperwork, I had come across it again.

I wasn't at all sure whether I wanted to risk looking at it. But finally curiosity took over, I put aside my apprehensions, gathered all my emotional courage, and studied the notes.

What I discovered created hours of puzzlement within me.

There were several pages with scribbles. The first page, the first line, showed from among the scribbles one clearly identifiable word: "yes." Further down the line there was a word that could be interpreted as either "son" or "soul." The next line, underneath that first one, couldn't be identified at all. The line under that one had one clearly identifiable word: "love" or perhaps "lovely." Then underneath that again unidentifiable scribbles, but a drawing that looked something like a flower.

The next page showed about six lines. The first one, after a few scribbles, had the word "number." The next line could be identified perhaps as "them" and then more scribbles. Line three, after scribbles, could be identified as "add" or "odd" and "wing."

The next line, emerging in the middle of the scribbles, had the word "wood," then some scribbles, then the word "women" clearly identifiable.

The next line showed nothing I could identify, and the last line again had a "yes" among the scribbles.

The last page, line one, the word "wood" again, the next line the words "we love you," and then again "wood."

Then there were notes of his latest dream—he even dated them. It was marked "Dreams—May '86." His date of death was July 7, 1986.

Dream one had the following notes: "The scaffolds, the great stone building—the guards—the whips—working as a grown man in ragged clothes on the timber scaffolds." There was a note that said: "(age 4 until 58—about five times)." I assume he meant he had the same dream five times during his lifetime.

Dream two: "The meat—wheeled cart—eating the meat and loading it. Getting on the seat, it's dark out. There's no electric light, it's very early medieval times, or earlier. Nailing the metal cover on the cart. (Only once, a very brief dream.)"

Dream three: "In the trenches in WW I, in no-man's-land, sticking my bayonet into a post to make a 'mark'—to leave some mark in the world that will be here after I'm gone— thinking while lying in a shell hole, 'I've not made any mark here on earth that will even show I've been here.'"

Well, my darling—my thoughts are racing—you *have* made a mark! In more than one way. Apart from the beautiful buildings (mostly churches) you have designed and that were built, there is the mark of your communication after death—the most profound of all. And now people will say that I've made all this communication up to set a monument for you. But you know that's not true. And so do I. The communication took place *before* I came across the notes.

But now I know more than I did before—or do I? Aren't there really more questions than answers now? Was the "automatic writing" a sort of premonition, a feeling of wanting to know his time? Or was it something like a subconscious projection of something hidden deep within? And what about the dreams? Was he, in past lives, something other than I knew him to be in this lifetime? On one of my evening walks I remember something he had told me in which I didn't place too much significance; it seemed too flattering to me. I had asked him if it was planned for him to leave when he did. He didn't answer my question directly, but told me that he had to leave before I did because even though he was more advanced in scholarly knowledge than I, I was "more abiding by the law of the universe," as he put it, and so he had to do some quick learning in the other world to catch up with me. He wants to be sure that when we plan our next life together, it will be even more harmonious and rewarding.

The initial shock over the discovery was wearing off, and

though I may not have found answers to all questions yet, perhaps day by day or year by year they will be given.

All has gone better than expected; Helen has been here with me for two weeks already, and so far it has been all right. The day before my trip to Florida to pick up Helen, a strange thing happened. Because of my busy work schedule, I try to take a quick afternoon nap. It refreshes my energies so that I can deal better with the heavy work load facing me each day. I napped on that day, too. For some reason I don't seem to remember any of my dreams during the last few years, but that day I awoke from a dream. It was a very short episode, but left me with a profound emotional feeling. I remember my concern about my planned trip and discussing it with someone—I couldn't quite determine who that was. It seemed not a person, but a force, invisible. But strong and loving. Somehow this force managed to calm my fears, and I awoke hearing myself say, "I shall do what is required." I felt good and comfortable after that. The next day I flew off to Florida to get Helen.

Before we left to come here, I had given Helen the message from her sister, "Tell my sister to quit the booze, or else she'll be dead in two years." She listened with an expression I could not quite identify—did she take it seriously, was she smiling inwardly, thinking, "Ah, baloney!" (with Helen one never knew!), or did she pretend it wasn't all *that* bad? After all, a few drinks a day, so what? Knowing Helen, I suppose I opted for that version.

It didn't really matter; I had no intention of making her promise something she couldn't keep (I knew better than that), although I would certainly try to coax her into joining AA.

Today she has finally unpacked most of her belongings. We have developed a reasonably comfortable routine. One benefit of her stay with me is that I'm seeing a bit more of Bob's family; his brother and family are visiting more often than before.

She gets up quite late in the morning—and why not. There aren't many tasks for her to do. I try to talk her into joining one of the local senior centers to have some activity, some diversion in her life. She agrees, but each time I want to take her, she finds a reason to postpone it. I know why; these activities take place either earlier in the morning, and she isn't ready to get up early, or later on in the afternoon, and that's when she has her drinks. Right on the dot at 3:00 p.m. she fixes herself a Scotch whiskey—she calls it "just one shot," but that shot fills a tall water glass! By 5:00 p.m. she is well "on the way," and at 6:00 p.m. we eat dinner. At 7:00 p.m. she is ready for bed. By now at least she is no longer taking sleeping pills—I firmly refused to be a part of that and told her in no uncertain terms that sleeping pills and alcohol just didn't mix.

She is a lot of fun in many ways. When she tells me incidents of her singing and dancing career, I break up with laughter. She has a good sense of humor, and the actress in her is able to relay that dramatically well. Helen is still quite beautiful—age has not damaged her physical beauty, and her charm is still abundant. The young generation of her family adores her, she is the personification of the stage character "Auntie Mame." But she can also be "a bit of a bitch," she herself admits. "Some people call me Hellion," she says with a naughty grin. Not too many people see that part of her; most of the time she is charm personified. She left a heartbroken older man in Florida, who would give his right arm to have her live with him.

Today I expect a visit from Frances, Aline, and a few other friends to introduce her to them. It turns out to be another one of life's surprises for me.

It's shortly after 3:00 when Aline and Frances arrive, the others aren't here yet. Helen has just had one of her drinks. I had been looking forward to their meeting Helen—Bob loved Helen very much, and naturally so do I.

As Frances walks into the room and I introduce Helen to

her, I can feel a surge of hostility weave through the room. It's almost as though an invisible wall of ice stands between them. Helen's first words (I am so shocked I don't remember what she says) are somewhat sarcastic and biting—she's lost all her charm, at least temporarily. I've never experienced anything quite like it and have absolutely no explanation for this. Aline has noticed some of the tension in the air, but graciously pretends it didn't happen and proceeds with the general small talk common to first introductory meetings.

In the meantime the others have arrived, and the afternoon proceeds reasonably smoothly.

After all have left and Helen has gone to bed, I say goodnight to Helen, as usual. Naturally I ask her what prompted her—to say the least—uncourteous behavior.

"Karma, I guess," she says.

I am surprised; so Helen also believes in reincarnation!

"Have you met in another life?" I ask, without showing my surprise.

"Oh, yes!" Helen exclaims with emphasis. "Oh, yes! She's cruel, you know. Very cruel."

Now I'm even more surprised: Frances cruel?! That's the most ridiculous thing I've ever heard!

"Come on, Helen—you've got to be kidding!"

"I am not! Absolutely not! She had me killed."

"When? What time period? How?" I'm glad no one can hear our conversation. They would certainly think the two of us had looked too deep into the bottle!

"I don't know when. All I remember is that she had ordered my execution."

"For what? In what capacity?" But Helen is silent now. "I'm tired," she says and is already half asleep. Naturally—the Scotch whiskey will do that. I'm also wondering whether it hasn't affected her rational thinking. On the other hand, these things are no longer so strange to me. It would be interesting to find out more about that.

Later on, via telephone, I ask Frances what she made of

this hostility toward her. She is not too clear herself, except that she also felt that there was something from a past life that would have influenced that behavior. But she couldn't remember anything at this time, she says.

All of this has never been cleared up—I was too busy to spend time pursuing these issues. I had enough on my hands to solve the problems of *this* lifetime. It was just very odd.

Time has gone by, and having Helen here with me is a mixed blessing; she is a link to Bob, in some way, but she also represents a physical and emotional task for me. The "shots" get bigger and more frequent, and with it her behavior becomes rambunctious at various times. Bill, Bob's brother, had stopped by several times to try to convince her to "quit the booze" and join AA, and she agreed; but when a specific time was set, she'd always find an excuse to back out of it.

It has become clearer and clearer to me that I couldn't be expected to spend the next decade or so under such circumstances. I feel I deserve better. But where would Helen go? Her friend in Florida is still begging her to come live with him—that would have to be the answer. Helen is complaining about cold weather conditions in this part of the country anyway. She keeps saying she misses the warm Florida sunshine. I wonder how she'll react when I suggest to her that perhaps it wouldn't be a bad idea to move back to Florida and live with her friend there.

She responds more favorably than I had dared hope for.

There is a family good-by dinner—Bill and Kathy have invited all of us out—and the next day I'm taking her to the airport. I see her leave with mixed emotions: part sadness, part relief.

Another phase of my life has come and gone. What I'm wondering about, though, is whether the message from her sister will come true; I hope not. At least I've done everything in my power to make it *not* materialize.

20

Back to the Burning Fountain

"... but the pure spirit shall flow
Back to the burning fountain whence it came.
A portion of the Eternal ..."

—Shelley

H elen's leaving from her brief encounter in my life has left a strange void. I've never been a person who couldn't be alone—too many things of interest in which to get involved—and as much as I love people and their company, there's also a need for time to reflect, to look inward, to ponder.

Even now, though, I cannot afford to look at Bob's photograph; seeing his kind, smiling face before me brings forth a powerful surge of longing for the physical presence and with it comes unbearable pain. As long as I can comfort myself with the metaphysical presence of the communication, I'm content and count my blessings that I have at least that.

171

Glimpses of Bob's last day, the day my life changed in the most profound way, have appeared on the horizon of my memory now and then like a dark cloud pronouncing lightning and thunder. Each time so far I've been able to dissolve them before they became too clear.

Today, for some strange reason (who can always know what triggers our memory) the day that took away my life's meaning—or so I thought then—July 7, 1986, has been permitted by my memory to become alive again. Perhaps it's a sign of the healing process that I let myself see, once again, what happened as though it were happening just now, this moment.

"Do you know," Bob says, all sweaty and tired-looking from painting the fascia board in front of the house, "can you believe it's already one year since our trip to Germany? I hate it when time flies so fast." He goes to the sink to wash himself off before taking a shower. "Boy, what a time *that* was." His eyes reflect with a dreamy look the vision of that memory.

"Yeah—and I bet you wish right now you were back there," I laugh. "It beats painting! But we're back on everyday living, my darling—we might as well adjust to that. Anyway, we just had the fourth of July, and I forgot to send Olivia a birthday card."

"What time are we supposed to be at Joann and Manucher's?" Bob continues. "I wish we could stay home, honey. I'm really quite pooped."

"Oh, you've got time to take a quick nap. You always fight going anywhere, and then once we're on the road you look forward to spending an evening with good friends, good conversation, good food. But something else, I wish you wouldn't paint outside in that heat—it really bothers me." I can't help but be a bit reproachful; we don't have much money, but we have enough to have some vinyl siding put up to avoid all that painting.

"Well, I like to keep busy in my retirement; it's good exercise."

I can't argue with that; Bob is a man who has to keep busy. And it *is* good exercise. Just not in the heat.

"True. But it's supposed to be 100 degrees today. Gosh, I hope they don't have the cookout outside today."

"If they do," says Bob, "I'll just say I want to go inside. I'm sure they'll all agree."

Before too long we're all cleaned up, dressed, and ready to go. I look at my handsome husband; he is seven years older than I am, but he is in such good shape and so good-looking! He is wearing a blue shirt and the phoenix bola tie he had wanted for his birthday. Before we leave to go to the party, I look at him. That blue shirt complements the color of his eyes, the silvery gray on his temples borders the lightly wavy hair, and his suntanned face makes him look the perfect picture of health. We arrive a little late (we always do!), but are greeted with great enthusiasm.

Joann and Manucher's parties are always fascinating. Manucher is from Iran and, of course, his many Iranian friends (and some family) are always present, as are Libby and Al, Bob's and my dear friends, who are Jewish. Bob and I find the mixture of different religious denominations intriguing. We don't seem to have any trouble liking each other, having fun together, respecting and cherishing each other.

During dinner Bob and I sit with different partners. I see that Bob is having an intense conversation with a very handsome Armenian man, who after dinner approaches me saying with great admiration, "Your husband is a very unusual man." He hands me a refill on my drink. "I've never come across an American who knows so much about my country; he knows our geography, our origin, our history, our customs—it's absolutely amazing."

"Yes," I reply with pride, "he is the most knowledgeable person I've ever come across. I don't know how he does it, knowing so much about everything. But his favorite subject is Egypt and perhaps Rome."

"Oh, yes," says the Armenian, "that *is* a fascinating subject: Egypt. I, too, could absorb myself in that."

We continue talking for a while longer, and then we mingle with others. Soon it's time to go home—it's about an hour's drive, and Bob and I are getting tired. Inside the air-conditioned house we had not felt the heat, but now, going outside to the car, the heat and humidity hit us like a hot, wet blanket.

The air is stale, heavy, and suffocating.

"My God," says Bob, "it's hard to breathe in this kind of weather. Thank God our car is air-conditioned."

"Yes, and our house, too," I add. "Or else I would try to sleep in someone's swimming pool!"

On the way home we turn the car radio on, exchange some of the various conversations we had had at the party, as we always do, and in no time at all we're home.

"I can't wait to read a bit more of Shirley MacLaine's book *Dancing in the Light,*" Bob says. It's our routine: we go to bed together, he reads for a while, and I go to sleep next to him in our king-sized bed.

Our German shepherd Hansi greets us with the usual loud enthusiasm. The cat Jezebel comes, purring, for her little bit of TLC. She is a Maine coon cat, who had found her way into our heart and home and decided to stay there! She seems to have been reared by raccoons; and her story was interesting enough that I wrote about her and had the article published in *Cats* magazine under the title "The Jezebel Mystery." We were sitting down for a while before going to bed, when Bob suddenly calls out, "Look, honey, look! Baby raccoons! The first ones this year!"

Excitedly we both go to the window, and there they are: two little fluff balls with their mother, curiously looking at us with their black button eyes, as if to say, "What kind of creature are *you?* You look funny to me."

Bob and I watch them for a few minutes, then we go to bed. Bob is reading, as he had said, *Dancing in the Light,* and before too long I have fallen asleep. I don't know how long I had slept, but suddenly I am awakened by a horrible sound. I am wide awake in an instant; I have heard that sound before.

I look at Bob; he is sitting in his usual position with his head against the headboard—but no, it's *not* the usual position: his head is too far backward, and the horrible sound is coming from his open mouth.

I race around to his side of the bed. Horror, indescribable horror, hits me in my guts. Quick! Quick! Something is wrong! No. No! It can't be. It is *not!* Oh, dear God—*no!* I try desperately to pull Bob into a lying-down position, but his body had turned to lead. Oh, God—am I doing the right thing—shouldn't I call 911? Phone! My God . . . the phone . . . can't think . . . where's the phone? Can't leave him, must revive . . . No, no, phone! *Phone!* Call for help!

I race to the other room to get the phone, trying to pull him down, in vain, trying to resuscitate anyway, while talking erratically to a voice on the other end. This isn't happening . . . It's a nightmare. I'm going to wake up in a minute. Yes, yes, I shall wake up . . . No, Bob, *no!* Don't!

Don't do this to me! Oh, please, God, please, You can't do this to me. You won't, will You? When the ambulance gets here, he'll wake up and smile at me and say, "Honey, what are you so worried about? Come on now; smile! I'm all right, see?" And all the time I'm working on him, not really knowing what I'm doing. My God, why can't I get him into the right position? I've always been so strong—where is my strength now when I need it?

Within a few minutes the ambulance is here. They take the limp body out of the house, work with some machines or instruments or both for quite a while, and then the ambulance disappears, after one of its personnel has told me the name of the hospital to which they are taking him. They ask if I want to come along, and I say no because I think they can work better without my presence. I'm numb. I don't know what I'm doing, except that I'm praying all the time, getting into the car like a robot. Where am I going? Ah, yes, to the hospital. There. Emergency room. The ambulance is there. He won't die. God will not let him die. Not yet. No. No. That won't happen. I go through the door. I sit down. Got to call the children. Phone.

Within a short while the children are there, Gloria and Ronnie. Pale. Horror on their faces.

A man in a white coat comes: "Mrs. Chesney, I'm sorry . . . !"

I don't hear what he says, but I know what it means. I *know.*

Pain . . . it's *not* a nightmare. It's real. O beloved Father, my Creator—do I still love You? When You give me so much pain? It's killing me, this pain! Well, just as well. I want to die anyway. Then the pain will go away. Perhaps I can *will* myself to die. Why can't I scream? I want to. I want this pain inside of me to flow out like a stream of heavy water.

Somehow I get home.

The children are there. Thank God for my children.

And there are Chris and Buck, and Monika and Roger, and Mama. Thank God for family.

I'm numb. Except for the pain. But I can't think. Why should I think? I'm going to be dead soon, too.

My life is over.

Life without my Bob *is* no life.

I hear Bob's voice saying—a long time ago—"Whoever will go first will contact the other."

But I don't believe it. I don't believe in anything any more.

Oh, I *hate* You, God! You give and then You take away. And You replace all that was good with a void, with pain. Why should I love You? You don't love *me!*

So why should I believe this thing about "life everlasting"—why? Life is a lie—we live just to end up with this horrible torture, this unbearable pain. And why couldn't it be *me* being dead—then I wouldn't have to go through all this.

Well, we shall see, You cruel Creator, You.

I'll try anyway, just to prove how wrong everything is.

Tomorrow morning I will try to make contact. It *is* tomorrow morning already.

Dawn has appeared.

I fall down on the couch.

21

The Elusive Golden Key

"Yet some there be that by due steps aspire
To lay their hands just on that golden key
That opes the palace
To Eternity."

—John Milton

It's hard to believe how quickly time goes by.

A little more than two years have passed since Bob left this realm of life. Hansi and I still take our evening walks, and I have begun, once again, to pay attention to everyday, ordinary events. In the beginning Bob had told me that he would be with me on a daily basis for about six months. When I was shocked hearing this (my life support seemed threatened) and I asked why not longer, he had replied that, after all, souls are also active on the other side—they don't just lie around in the "Garden of Eden" doing nothing. I could detect a slight trace of gentle sarcasm, as though he had expected me to know better. Well, perhaps I did, but I didn't want to face any disruption of communication. It frightened me.

Then, after about eight months, when we still communicated on a daily basis, I asked him why the communication was still active. "Nothing is carved in stone," he said, and I could sense a little smile. But before too long it started to slow down to a few times a week, then only now and then when absolutely needed. One example: Driving home one day from an outing with our grandchildren, in heavy traffic, something triggered a very strong memory, and the longing for his presence became so powerful that I feared for the safety of my driving. The pain of loss hit me once again with tremendous force—so much so that I was getting ready to pull over to the side and cry, but I fought the urge because I didn't want the children upset.

Suddenly I heard his beloved voice again: "Honey, please don't. Have you forgotten everything I told you? That I *am* with you? That I will help you always? That my love is yours forever, regardless of where I am? Remember the saying, 'O ye of little faith'? Have faith, my darling, please, have faith."

I immediately felt all right again. Once again a soothing ointment had been layered over my pain.

Now I hardly ever hear from him—and that's all right. It's very strange, though; it's almost as though I'm eternally connected. When needed, I hear from him—as though an energy line within myself has been attached to the unknown dimension of life, where he exists. The occurrences in my life take place on a normal basis, the usual struggles and problems common to all earthly existence. But "when the going gets rough" (and it has, much more so than I wish), I hear him comfort me, support me, so that it almost feels like an everyday occurrence. I'm no longer sure whether this is my drawing on memories from the past, having known him so well, having been so close. Margaret had once said, when I mentioned some of these quandaries to her, "I don't think it matters. We know too little about the time factor.

Past, present, future: what do we *really* know about that? The important fact is, it happens. And that it helps. And so, who cares?" I had laughed a little.

Perhaps, if I had wanted to be a so-called "channel" for receiving information from "the other side," I would still be hearing profound things—but I want to live a more uncomplicated life. Getting information on different subject matters can become complex. Everyday living has become very complicated for me, and I just want to live in relative normalcy for at least a short while—just enough to recover from all the turmoil that seems to find its way to me.

Perhaps, some day, I shall be open again for different kinds of communication. But somehow it has become clear to me that though I may have choices, the direction of my life is handled by someone else. What will be, will be. I'll try to do the best I can with the circumstances as they present themselves. I always have.

Hansi has begun to be a source of worry for me; he is approaching thirteen years of age, and his health, which had never been too good, is failing. I dread another loss. Not yet, I tell myself, please, not yet—knowing all the time that it will have to happen. It's just a matter of time. But I take it a day at a time.

Today I visited my friend Hilde. She and her husband always give me a warm welcome, and they're among those of my friends who are protective of my well-being. Mike, a young friend of their daughter's, had also come to visit, and since Mike has a similar route, he offered to take me home.

Mike and I have developed a very special relationship; his mind is always searching for answers to questions about science, the universal workings, the unknown; and his intelligence is always open to tackling another mystery. Whenever I've had get-togethers with my group of friends, he had always been among them, adding a great deal of insight and information to the conversation.

During a previous get-together I had told Mike about a recent incident concerning communication with Bob.

One Sunday morning I had awakened at 6:00 feeling Bob's presence. I had asked him why I hadn't heard from him for so long, and he said he'd been busy. "Busy doing what?" I asked. He gave me only two words: "matrix calculus."

That had startled me. I had heard the expression *calculus* and had a general idea as to its meaning, but I had no idea what *matrix* meant. I got up and looked up both words in the dictionary. Under *matrix* it said: "That which gives form or origin to a thing, or which serves to enclose it, or: a formative part, or the intercellular substance of a tissue, or: the womb, or: the rock in which a crystallized substance is embedded, or: a mold for casting type faces," and so on. Under *calculus* only a few explanations seemed to fit: "A method of calculation, especially a highly systematic method of treating problems by a special system of algebraic notation. See differential, infinitesimal, and integral calculus."

I was absolutely stunned; I had no scientific education. Granted, I was interested in such matters—but to wake up at 6:00 in the morning with a scientific, highly complex quotation!

What was Bob trying to tell me? Was he trying to say that around us, within the universal existence, events are taking place that we can hardly comprehend, but should be aware of? How can we be aware of something we don't understand? Thinking about what I had heard, though, gives me *some* insight—too complex to fully develop the thought; nevertheless, the important word in this message was the word *matrix*. Was it meant to refer to creation? It seemed to be the only thing to make sense.

I conceived a small inkling of something more to come. When I had told Mike about this incident, he was fascinated. "My God, Inga," he had said with awe, "do you know what that means? It means you could get answers to questions humanity has been searching for over a period of decades."

I hadn't answered. If I was honest with myself, I had to admit that the thought frightened me. I didn't *want* to be a so-called "channel" for whatever information. Too much responsibility—and perhaps too much mental work! Besides, there was the danger of interference from the "dark side," the negative forces. How could I ever be sure that the information was not misleading, or something . . . ? No, I didn't want to deal with that—all I wanted was to hear my Bob tell me that love was forever.

Tonight, though, on the way home, the subject has come back to life. After Mike and I have talked for a while about exploring the unknown, he says, "Do you think, Inga, that you're on a one-to-one basis of communication with Bob?"

I hesitate for a few seconds. "I don't know, Mike. I believe I am. But I can't be sure if that is the case *all* the time, nor whether my communication with him is not, at times, a projection of my own need to hear from him."

"Why don't you make sure," Mike says. We're almost home.

"Well, how do you suggest I do that?" I'm curious now.

"Simple. Just ask him a direct question, letting him know you expect a direct answer."

"Such as?"

"You could ask if the universe is symmetrical," Mike says, as though the answer to that is the simplest thing in the world!

I almost laugh out loud. If I *would* get an answer, I wouldn't even be able to comprehend it, let alone transcribe it correctly into my diary!

Instead, I just place this whole disturbing request on the light side, "Mike, you've got to be kidding. It's late, I'm dead tired, and even if I were to get an intelligent answer, I wouldn't know what to do with it."

"Yes, you would," he says simply.

"Well, you're nice to have such confidence in me. But some other time—perhaps. Not tonight. My mind is tired. I am tired."

We say good-night, and after he's left I take Hansi for his walk. I'm determined not even to *think* "symmetry" and "universe."

The evening walk is routine. Bob and I exchange a few loving words, and I feel I've been quite successful in avoiding the issue of the direct question.

I go to bed, very tired but comfortable.

And then it happens.

I am already half asleep, when I hear Bob's voice. In a flash I'm wide awake, because I hear the word *symmetry.* I run to get paper and pencil, and I'm writing down what I'm hearing.

"Symmetry cannot be applied to any concept in the cosmos," I hear Bob say. "It's strictly a concept for human understanding, since it's a *dimensional* concept. Humans know of only three dimensions, but there are ten in cosmic concept (or law)." (I had the distinct feeling that Bob wanted to say "twelve" instead of "ten" dimensions; why I wrote down only "ten" I really don't know. I have no explanation for this.) Bob continues: "Einstein came close to knowing six dimensions, but had too many obstacles in the human body and life to fully concentrate."

"What were the dimensions?" I ask.

"Space, speed, vision, sound, balance, and gravity."

I debate: "But we do know these six."

"Yes—but not in the form of unity."

"Unity?" I ask, puzzled.

"Volume," Bob says. And then he concludes, "Enough for today."

Needless to say, sleep is far away tonight. I am totally overwhelmed. Bob has given me a puzzle that may take years to solve.

Once again I pick up the dictionary. I have never thought

of balance or gravity as dimensions—but what about modern scientists? Is some information going to be discovered that may deal with the origin of the universe? The "big bang" theory? If so, I certainly will not be able to solve this puzzle; the scientific community will have to do that. And the scientific community will probably laugh at my information, especially at the way I received it.

Now to see what *volume* really means.

It says, "The size, measure, or amount of anything in three dimensions: cubic magnitude; gases expanding to a greater volume; mass or quantity, especially a large quantity of anything; the volume of sound, to pour out volumes of abuse," and various other explanations.

What I had heard certainly sounds as though it may have to do with creation or the "big bang." It's frustrating to realize that with my limited educational background I will never be able to solve this puzzle. My instincts tell me, that there is a valuable answer hidden there. Oh, that Bob! Why doesn't he just come out and say: "This is the way it was," and then give me a scientific formula! And it's almost as though he hears me and chuckles and says, "But, honey—then it wouldn't be any fun!" On the serious side, though, some time ago he had told me that existence on "the other side" does not entitle one to "power" over others—in other words, the natural course of events cannot be directed by "them" or altered or changed in any way. "We can introduce thoughts into people's minds," Bob had said. "That's all. They themselves make the decisions, but sometimes by our introducing a new way of thinking, people can make a better decision."

I have pondered enough over all of this. Perhaps some day there'll be a clearer answer for me, too.

In the meantime there are good moments, then sad moments, and sometimes moments of mixed emotions.

My son Ron and his wife had a baby while Bob was still

alive. This little girl is her parents' pride and joy. Bob and Kristin enjoyed each other's company. She would climb up on his lap, and he would draw little faces on her fingernails—much to her delight.

She couldn't fully understand about death at her age, but I could tell that she missed him.

A few days ago we had gone to a picnic at Eric McKeever's house; there was a "treasure hunt" for the children. She was eagerly participating in the hunt, but became very subdued and quiet on the way home. I asked what was wrong, and she started crying. "Grandpa wasn't there," she sobbed.

I stopped the car. I remembered the last time we were there, Bob had been present. Had she expected to find Grandpa among the hidden treasures?

I had to swallow the lump in my throat that almost choked me.

"But he *was* there, Kristin," I said. "You just couldn't see him."

"Why not? Doesn't he want me to see him?"

I wiped her tears. "Oh, it's not like that at all, honey," I said, trying to suppress my own tears. "It's just that where he is now, he is so busy he can only spare a few moments for us now and then, but he knows he is right inside your heart, and he will always be there. That makes him feel good, knowing that. So you keep on thinking about him now and then, and remember all the wonderful things we did together, because he does remember that, too. And then he's very happy. Do you think you'll do that?"

She nodded, her little face quite serious. Then she looked into her treasure bag. "Maybe Grandpa put that in there," she said, now smiling again.

"Who knows?" I smiled along with her.

Alita and Erika, Gloria's two daughters, miss Bob, too, but they are teen-agers and more in control of their feelings, at least on the outside. I have told them all about my experience with communication, but cannot tell whether they believe it to be "real" or not. They are good children, a joy to their parents and me.

Life has been good in spite of my need for Bob's physical presence. My friends and I meet at least once a month to talk about spiritual matters, and each time they leave, a sense of well-being stays behind.

Going to church is becoming more and more of a joy. We have a new minister who knows exactly how to reach people to relay the message of faith.

But I know I'm soon going to have to face one more profound loss: Hansi. His health is failing quickly. Recently he was in the hospital for one week; when I brought him home, I counted my blessings, hoping and praying to keep him just a bit longer.

Somehow, though, my inner feeling tells me it's just a matter of time. But I can't face that, not yet.

When the time comes, God will help me to cope.

22

Appreciation and Reflections

A nother Christmas season is approaching—another one without Bob. But this time I'm home! As usual, the plan is to spend Christmas Eve at my sister and brother-in-law's house where my mother lives. It's always wonderful to be with the whole family; it's quite a crowd! We draw names; otherwise, the activity of gift-giving and unwrapping would take the whole evening. The children, in order to participate fully in the Christmas spirit, are encouraged to produce a little skit or recite a poem. They do it with enthusiasm; they have a good audience to appreciate their talent and work.

Erika, Gloria's youngest daughter, is a member of a band;

she plays the flute, as her older sister had done; and the school has arranged for the usual Christmas concert. The performance is always a joy; the youngsters are good at what they do. The band has won several prizes in band contests. Going to the concert means a temporary diversion from everyday tasks and problems. I can immerse myself fully in the music. It's lovely.

Then, for a few moments, my memory awakens again. I feel a great deal of sadness that Bob and I had so little time to attend the musical functions that took place during Gloria's school years. We missed out on something wonderful; Gloria was in the school choir, and she had a beautiful voice.

With a sense of regret I look at the stage, thinking about Bob, Gloria, Ronnie, and the years we had together.

My thoughts go to Gloria and Roy, her husband. As with most couples, the two of them in their first three years of marriage have had their struggles to get used to each other's little idiosyncrasies. The latest incident was one of major disturbance—at least, so it seemed. I can't help but think about them, sending a silent prayer for help in resolving their differences. Then I decide that perhaps that isn't quite enough—maybe I should do more. Before my eyes I picture each one of them under a cross of light which is hovering over their heads and then include in the group my two grandchildren, and then Ron and his family—all of them under this cross of light.

I have never before felt compelled to do anything quite like it.

Suddenly the group of about fifty teen-agers on stage with their musical instruments disappears from my vision, and instead I see only a small group of about five, which then disappears also, leaving a small round area of subdued light. Suddenly, within that circle I see Bob and his mother! Just the faces, not the bodies.

I am elated. It's the first time Bob has ever appeared to

me in vision, instead of just a voice. I'm not quite sure why his mother is there with him, but it doesn't matter! It lasts only a few minutes, then the vision disappears, and I'm fully aware again of my surroundings.

I am slightly shaken up. What does that mean? But then, I don't care. It was wonderful to see Bob instead of hearing only his voice!

On my way home from the concert that feeling of joy is still with me.

As I enter the house, I see there's a message on my telephone recorder. It's Gloria; her voice sounds not at all as usual. Earlier during the day when I last talked to her, her voice was cold—now I can hear the timber of emotional warmth and uproar. "Mom, please call me," the message says. "It's urgent." She sounds as though she's been crying.

I immediately call.

"Mom, you wouldn't believe what a strange day this has been," there's a tremble in her voice, and it sounds as though she's been crying. "First of all, when did you put that newspaper clipping in the book?"

I had given Roy a book to give to Gloria. She had given it to Bob as a present some years ago, and as I was cleaning out the basement where we had more bookshelves, I decided that Gloria should enjoy it. It was her favorite author. But I hadn't placed any newspaper clipping in it!

"What clipping?" I ask her, surprised.

"The article from the *SunPaper* dated 1984," she says. "You mean you didn't put it there?"

"Absolutely not. What's the article about?"

She is silent for a while. "The article describes me and my situation," she says, with even more of a tremble in her voice. "Dad must have put it there some years ago."

"Yes, but for it to get to you *now*," I say, "that's really something. Of all the books I could have chosen, to choose *that* one."

"That's not all, Mom. When Roy and I were home tonight,

we heard Sarah" (their dog) "bark and bark, and she wouldn't stop. Now you know, she doesn't usually bark. We couldn't quite understand it, but thought that perhaps there were other dogs roaming around outside, so we ignored it.

"But after a while we did get concerned, and Roy walked outside to see whether everything was all right. He saw a police car four houses away. He walked toward it, and the officer told him that there had been an 'incident.' The woman of the house, quite pregnant, had to face an intruder with a ski mask and a gun, who robbed her of whatever valuables there were. She was alone—her husband was away on a business trip. She was very frightened, needless to say. Well, Roy and I realized that most likely the robber had our house in mind, since it was the closest to the road. That's why Sarah was barking so much, but it must also have deterred him and he decided to try somewhere else. Who knows, since there were two of us, in our case it may have turned out quite differently." Her voice quivers as she continues, "But you know—it *did* have a good effect on Roy and me; we realized that we were so lucky to have each other, have our health and beautiful home. Both of us cried, and then we hugged each other."

When I asked about the time period of the event, it became clear that it coincided with my experience of seeing Bob and his mother and placing the cross of light above their heads during the concert.

Thank you.

We can wish and pray for miracles. They do happen.

Christmas Eve is here. Once again we're all together. I have to fight the urge to concentrate too much thinking about Bob—it's still too touchy. I don't want to cry and make everybody else sad.

Rose, my sister's daughter, after the first onslaught of gift-giving and celebrating, motions everyone to be quiet for a moment. Then she says, ceremoniously, "Aunt Inga, we all wanted to give you something special for Christmas, something that would include Uncle Bob. Here it is."

She gives me an envelope. It contains the photograph of a lion in the Baltimore Zoo and announces that the lion has been "adopted" for one year by Mr. Robert William Chesney. It was a program the zoo offered the public in order to get donations for improving conditions of wildlife in the zoo.

I am deeply touched, and now it's even harder for me to suppress my tears. I'm not quite successful in doing so, but soon the hustle and bustle of the crowd takes over, and everything is reasonably back to normal.

A few days later I go to the zoo to visit "our" lion.

It's a beautiful animal, majestic and proud.

God has created a lovely world.

23

Pilgrims of Mortality

"For a moment of night we have a glimpse of our-selves and of our world islanded in its stream of stars—pilgrims of mortality, voyaging between hori-zons across the eternal seas of space and time."

—Henry Beston

The day has come. I know I must act. Hansi's medical treatment is no longer effective, his whole system is failing. I don't know if he's in pain, but I know he's no longer happy. He always loved his food—now he will not eat, as though he's resigned himself to departure.

My extensive discussions with the veterinarian have convinced me that there is no hope for recovery. "When animals start losing control over their bodily functions," the veterinarian had said, "they lose their dignity, and then they suffer." Apart from that, I can hardly watch him die of starvation. I don't believe in keeping him alive just for my peace of mind, especially knowing that it won't be for long anyway.

I want Hansi to go to the other realm of life right here, at home, where he was always so happy.

The day is filled with sunshine, and within my heart I try to see the light beyond, but it's difficult for me to see through the dark cover of my emotions. Once again, as the last time in July, a chain saw is cutting up my heart.

Hansi, the veterinarian, and I have gone outside to sit down on the lawn. I try not to cry: Hansi would always get upset when he saw me crying over something. But I have no control over it.

As the anesthesia slowly enters his body, Hansi suddenly lifts his head and places it on my knee, keeping it there. His head is resting on my knee like a jewel, protected by the gentle embrace of an open palm.

Then I hear a contented little sigh, as though he's saying, "Ah, that feels so good . . . thank you . . . " and he's asleep.

The veterinarian has something moist glistening in his eyes and hurries away.

I go inside the house to call my son Ron, and within a few minutes he is there. Together we place Hansi in his grave. I say a prayer, and then I have to fight the desire to leave this world, as I did when Bob left. The peace on the other side is so tempting—compared to the chain saw cutting away at my heart. I want it to stop, but it doesn't.

Ron stays with me for as long as he can, but he has to go to work.

Unexpectedly, after a few hours, the pain has decreased. Every time the chain saw wants to cut, I see Hansi's head on my knee, I hear his sigh of contentment, and I am all right.

The veterinary hospital placed no charge for that day.

Now that companion is gone, too.

And still life goes on. But sometimes we get weary.

A few days have gone by, and I find a letter from the veterinary hospital in the mail: "A gift in memory of Hansi has been received from the Animal Medical Clinic Dulaney Valley. The Animal Medical Clinic sent a cash gift in memory of

Hansi to Morris Animal Foundation. This thoughtful contribution will help sponsor studies to improve companion animal health and brighten the future of dogs everywhere.

"It's always hard to lose a companion like Hansi, but this generous gift helps assure that future generations will benefit from Hansi's memory."

It would be wrong of me to be sad when I'm surrounded by so much caring, so many good people. I'm fortunate.

Naturally, Bob's presence had been there—assuring, helping, supporting. One afternoon, sitting outside on the patio, we talked about "the animal kingdom." He assured me once again that animals do have souls, though theirs is a separate kind of "kingdom" and runs on a different principle. I had a hard time connecting to that thought—it created conflicting emotions. The thought of Hansi being in good care was one I loved hearing, but what about domestic animals killed for food? Or hunted animals? Bob told me that this *was* the difference; since animals do not have humanity's brain capacity, they're not consciously aware of death; they function in the body purely on instinct, with minor differences among the species. Therefore, on a very limited basis, some species recognize a little more than others. Some are capable of feeling love, fear, dislike, like, desire, caution, and so on. Others are functioning on a very primitive survival basis. But there is some very minor soul development also and a chance for furthering that. The difference between their and human soul levels is that cognitive abilities depend on mental capacity. They were created at the same time as humans, but had a weaker constitution during creation, some kind of "creative flaw"; and since nothing is wasted in nature, their use was determined to help support life or just serve for enjoyment of humans or serve some other tasks.

I asked if they, too, may choose to return in another body at another time. "Sometimes," Bob had said. "You have to remember that there are vast differences among the species and don't forget the cognition factor. With animal souls there are *vast* differences, and all of this is on a *very* limited basis. Their creative purpose is to serve *humankind*, while the human's creative purpose is to serve *God*."

I should have asked why then do creatures who serve humans need a soul; wouldn't just a body suffice? But since I wanted to put all this down in writing, I felt now was not the time. Later on, I decided that the answer probably was contained in the statement that they, too, were *created* as souls. With slight imperfections, I noted with a chuckle. Somewhat like a subsidy now to humankind.

The explanation that Bob had given me made me happy. Nothing good is ever wasted in God's creation, and Hansi *is* a good soul.

Another six months have passed.

It is the morning of March 13, and as I'm looking at the calendar, I realize that tomorrow is our wedding anniversary.

I see Bob sitting in his beloved leather armchair, holding baby Kristin on his lap.

I see him sitting at his desk working late at night on a side job for extra money, having spent most of the evening helping Gloria and Ron with their school homework. He looked so tired, yet there was no complaint.

I see him up on the roof with a bucket of tar, repairing a leak. It saved money—we didn't have much of that.

I see him all flustered and gravely concerned when I wasn't feeling well, almost driving me crazy with his concern.

I see him sitting outside with his constant cup of coffee and a cigarette, enjoying the leisure.

I hear his hearty laughter coming from deep within, with that little tinge of mischievousness, during visits from our children, and all the good-natured teasing that went on.

I remember all the intellectual conversations and debates we had—alone and with friends.

I remember his flexible, open mind and his multiple hobbies: archaeology, history, geology, searching for answers on old and new problems, politics, the universe, religion.

And I remember his caresses and the look of love radiating from his eyes toward me, and the feeling of total contentment he gave me through his presence. And the recognition of loss is once again piercing my heart like a sword, and anger rises like a fountain: *I want my husband! I want him here! Now!* Not at some distant future in another world! Do you hear me, God?! *Now!*

My sobbing accompanies my silent, furious rebellion.

And then I feel ashamed. O God, forgive me, please. What am I saying? At least I *did* have twenty-two years of happiness.

The ringing of the telephone diverts me from my thoughts. It's Frances.

"Something strange just happened, about fifteen minutes ago," she says. "I was downstairs in the kitchen, when I heard all the doors upstairs bang shut. I thought it very strange, since there really wasn't enough of a breeze to cause such a loud closing of doors. I went upstairs to check it out, but could not find any reason for it. So I went downstairs again and was standing at the dishwasher, when I heard the only door downstairs squeak. Now, that door *had been closed!* I went to take a look and saw Oliver the cat look at the door as though he saw something. *The door had opened!* Now, for some reason I thought about Bob." She laughs apologetically as she continues, "You know, Inga, it's not that I don't think about Bob now and then, but I don't think about him that often."

"I would think that very strange," I tease her. "But it seems to me that perhaps he's trying to tell you that the old doors are closing, and a new door is opening," I continue, knowing that she's anxious to hear news about a new, important position at a local college that she's applied for. She's sitting on pins and needles to hear from them. "Who knows—maybe you'll hear from them soon."

"That would be nice," she sighs. "It certainly would be nice."

Later on that day she calls me back. "Guess what?" She's jubilant. "Guess what, they called me today. I have an interview on Tuesday!"

"See? I told you Bob was trying to tell you something."

"Yeah! Let him keep on that way!" she laughs.

We talk about her future for a few more minutes, and then she says. "Oh, there's something else rather strange. After that marvelous phone call, I went shopping, and as I returned home in my car, with the windows open since it was such a beautiful, warm, sunshiny day, I suddenly heard someone whistle. But you know where I live and so you know also that on that road you can easily see if someone is nearby or not. There was not *one* person in sight! It was a lovely simple little tune, and I was sure I would remember it—but, you know, I don't remember any part of it."

We talk for a few more minutes, and then we proceed with the tasks of the day.

That evening, sitting outside on the patio, I suddenly find myself whistling.

The first tune is a funny little German folk song: "Ach du lieber Augustin." And I know that's not it. The next tune hits home; I *know* this is it! It's an old German love song: "Ach, wie ist's möglich dann, dass ich dich lassen kann; hab' dich von Herzen lieb, dass glaube mir . . . Du hast die Seele mein so ganz genommen ein, dass ich kein' andern lieb, als dich allein . . . "

As I'm whistling this tune, a surge of emotions races through me, comforts me, huddles itself around me once again like that blanket of emotional velvet.

The translation would be something like, "Oh, how impossible it is to let go of you . . . I love you with all my heart, that you must believe . . . you are within my soul, so that I'll never be able to love anyone else but you . . . "

Once again there's that lump in my throat, but this time it's one of happy sentiment. Still, I must find out if that's the tune Frances heard.

I go inside and call Frances. "Would you recognize that tune if I whistled it?"

"I think so," she says.

I whistle "Ach du lieber Augustin."

"No," she says without hesitation. "That's not it."

I whistle the second tune, the love song.

"Hmmm, I'm not sure. Do it again."

I repeat the tune.

"Yes," she says, with slight uncertainty, "do it again, but just a bit faster."

I comply.

"Yes! That's it! That's definitely it," she says with enthusiasm.

"Are you sure?"

"Of course, I'm sure! You know me well enough by now to know that, Inga."

She's right. In her profession as a professor at a college she can't afford guesswork.

"But what's that all about?" she asks.

I fill her in on the latest events. And then I say, "Frances, do you know what that means? It's my anniversary present! He *had* to choose a third person, so that I would believe. And it had to be a tune that you had never heard before, but he and I knew. Bob didn't know that many German songs, but he knew that one. I had played it on the accordion many times. Not many Americans know the words to that song; it's a rather old one. O God, isn't that wonderful?"

"It's incredible," she says. "He knew I would tell you. He knew I wouldn't know that tune, but that *you would,* and you would recognize it and check back with me, and between the two of us we'd figure it out. It's almost too much to handle."

"Not for me!" I jubilate. "Not for me! My anniversary tomorrow will be wonderful!"

O, my love, my heart, my soul, my transformation, my connection to that which is, has been, and always will be. Thank you, God. The gifts You give are spectacular.

Today I'm playing the tape from the Jesus time period again. This time Doris wants to hear it. But Aline and Frances are also here; they had said they wanted to hear it again, too.

The playing time is about ninety minutes. The "big room" is once again filled with the warm, spiritual softness surrounding a circle of caring, good, loyal, and unselfish people.

Doris has her eyes closed—she is absorbing all of it with relaxed concentration. Frances and Aline also look relaxed.

Once in a while Doris asks me to pause the tape, and I comply. Then she asks a question or requests to have a certain portion of it replayed, and we continue.

After the tape is finished, we talk about the subject for a while. "I can't help it," I say to my friends, "but something is working in the back of my mind—I don't quite know what it is. Maybe it's what Bob had told me months before I decided to have this hypnosis session: that I was 'touched by the star of Bethlehem.'" I had told no one else but my three closest friends. I know they would not think me strange. "What do you think he could have meant by that? I'll never forget how it had irritated me. I couldn't figure out if he was making fun of me. But then, Bob doesn't do that—not about something so important and intimate. I don't understand it."

Frances laughs. "My God, girl," she says with that gentle informed assuredness that is so typical of her personality. "Don't you *know* what that means? I'm surprised—I thought you knew."

Now I'm surprised. "No—I *don't* know." I'm almost a little

irritated again; how come I don't know? "I'm surprised that *you* think you know." I didn't want to sound irritated. I hope I didn't. "Do you think I was born at the same hour as Jesus or something like that?"

"Has nothing to do with that," she says, now very serious. "Nothing at all. My God, Inga, it's so obvious that it surprises me that you didn't figure it out; Bob meant 'star' not as an interpretation in the sense of physics, like constellations or so, but in the context of Hollywood, as in *movie star.*" She gives me a few minutes to absorb it. Then she says, with that subdued, quiet importance, "The 'Star' of Bethlehem was Jesus."

Time has gone by, and the wounds of living the battle of life are healing. They always do. Those that don't are those we ourselves have inflicted upon our soul. We are our own pupil, our own teacher, our own judge. We have the right to make decisions, but we must also be willing to live with the consequences of our decisions.

In the final analysis it doesn't matter what happens to us, but how we *deal* with our fate.

We can regress, or we can advance.

We can die, or we can live.

Every day there is a light shining somewhere; we just have to look for it, let it enter our heart, and keep it warmly lit with all the things that are good.

When we turn away from our pain, our misfortunes, our losses, and concentrate on something positive, the healing process starts.

In the face of that something that we cannot understand, that mysterious concept called eternity, death is only one thing: death is the *nothing,* the *void.* But that need not be there, when *life* is available to us. I am grateful for a love that once was mine—knowing that life means more than we could possibly imagine and that God will not abandon us, unless we ourselves create the disconnection.

We were given vision—but we can only see as far as our vision permits. What wonders we could perceive if we expanded our vision!

Perhaps the true magic hidden among all the events after Bob died is the recognition that *all* of it was a song of love, sent from beyond the realm of earthly existence.

All of us have the ability to hear the music, if we just turn the radio on.

I shall keep on listening—with gratitude.

24

Final Thoughts

S even years have passed since Bob died, and life has made sure I was going to be kept busy and presented with challenge after challenge. Now and then—as time permits—discussions concerning the subjects presented on the preceding pages reappear on the horizon of my life, like a rainbow of varying colors.

One year ago Helen died of cirrhosis of the liver. There had been many telephone calls from Florida, and more than once I wanted to go visit her, but she always said, "Not yet, maybe later." And I knew it was because she was aware that being a caregiver to my mother, who had had a massive stroke and was quite dependent upon everyday care, would limit my ability to travel anywhere. These were tormented times; I loved Helen and wanted to be with her. I often thought about the "message"—could fate have been changed somewhat? Perhaps not; life is what it is—we have free will. When I look back at all events, they seem no more unreal now than they did then.

Eric McKeever, Bob's closest friend, had given me the Edgar Cayce biography *There Is a River* by Thomas Sugrue, and I had read it with total fascination. I also wondered why Bob and I had not read it; of all the reading material, this would have been the most obvious in which to absorb ourselves. Perhaps there was so much to choose from that we overlooked the apparent. But now this book presented me with some answers.

Sugrue says that "Edgar told [a] story to illustrate the truth that when any person who is habitually an objective thinker begins to experiment with subjective thinking, he sees and hears strange things and imagines he is having psychic experiences. 'Actually, he is only meeting the reality of himself,' Edgar explained."

Had I "met the reality of myself," and if so, had it influenced my encounters, my perceptions?

When, some time ago, my friend Mike asked me to place the question to Bob as to whether the universe was symmetrical or not, I tried to avoid doing that, but the answer came anyway. Prompted by my subconscious? Perhaps, but I doubt it.

I've spent a few moments now and then during the last few years trying to analyze what I had heard: Did it make any sense at all? And why did it happen?

Every answer to the information Bob had relayed to me, especially the words about dimensions, symmetry, and so on seemed much of a guessing game. Also, there was little sense in searching for answers—there could hardly ever be any proof about correctness or incorrectness. Still, much of what we believe is based on assumptions: the thought, the idea precedes the search for proof. Now here was someone who many years before my own experience has encountered similar thoughts, perceptions, deductions. With a great deal of pleasure (and curiosity) I absorbed myself in connecting the author's findings to what I had heard Bob say several years ago and tried to bring some kind of sense into it.

The key word was *dimensions.*

Bob had said that there were actually ten dimensions, and I had had the feeling that he had wanted to say twelve. In the Cayce biography on page 311 it says, "The planets of the solar system represent the dimensions of consciousness of the system—its consciousness as a whole. There are eight dimensions to the consciousness of the system." If I add "unity" and "volume" to Bob's specific mention of six dimensions, then I have eight. The other two—or four?— I felt he had wanted to mention are still a mystery.

Reading the Sugrue book explained to me the six dimensions. Bob had mentioned: "space, speed, vision, balance, gravity, and sound."

When I had said that we already knew of these (though perhaps some of them not exactly in the dimensional sense), Bob had said, "But not in the form of unity." Upon my puzzlement he had added, "Volume—enough for today."

I had pondered over this for a long time. Somehow I had the feeling that Bob had given me an explanation of creation, but usually ended up too tired from my rather involved and demanding life to be able to piece it together entirely. Now and then I tried to comprehend some of the scientific programs on TV debating the "big bang" theory, implosion and explosion, black holes, quantum mechanics, and so on, but my scientific education was next to zero. At times I sensed more than I could explain, but it left me still pondering.

Now here seemed to be someone who confirmed and

explained what I had sensed.

Moreover, it explained Bob's very first communication with me: the word *symphonies*. It seemed to tie everything together in a rather neat package.

On page 307 of the Sugrue book it says, "The cosmos was built with the tools which man calls music, arithmetic, and geometry: harmony, system, and balance. The building blocks were all of the same material, which man calls the life essence. It was a power sent out from God, a primary ray, as man thinks of it, which by changing the length of its wave and the rate of its vibration became a pattern of differing forms, substance, and movement. This created the law of diversity which supplied endless designs for the pattern. God played on this law of diversity as a person plays on a piano, producing melodies and arranging them in a symphony."

Symphony!

That was the word Bob had given me at the very first moments of our communication after his death, and I had doubted my sanity when I heard it! How easily, given enough time and patience, we find answers.

The book said much more that tied in exactly with what Bob told me.

Yet for my own human linear thinking it was still difficult to piece all of this together in a way that would make logical sense to me. I had to ask myself some more questions.

Could the dimensions Bob had named or the eight mentioned in the Cayce biography really be considered dimensions? So far humans had been able to deal with a three-dimensional concept, nothing more. I looked up the word *dimension* in the dictionary.

It said: "Magnitude measured in a particular direction, or along a diameter or principal axis; measure, extent, size, magnitude." That would certainly apply to sound, balance, speed, and gravity—they *can* be measured. But what about "vision" and "space"?

The explanations for *vision* in the dictionary are profoundly varied in scope, and all of them can apply to the concept of dimensions—in fact, they broaden the view.

That leaves *space.*

Nothing could be more dimensional than space. It encompasses *everything.* The dictionary says, "The unlimited or indefinitely great general receptacle of things, commonly conceived as an expanse extending in all directions (or having three dimensions) in which, or occupying portions of which, all material objects are located."

Three dimensions are mentioned in the dictionary. Bob stated there were ten, of which he named six, and the Cayce biography mentions eight. I believe that some day, far in the future, the dictionary will have to be updated! For now, assuming that Bob's information is correct, I shall concentrate on combining the six he gave me to a *whole.*

If all six (I can only connect the six, since it's not clear from the Sugrue book what the other two might be) are combined into one, then we have the workings of the universe, of which the human body, mind, and spirit are a part. Perhaps each individual life form is a little universe. That would explain Bob's statement "in the form of *unity.*"

The explanation in the dictionary of "the size, measure or amount of anything in three dimensions; cubic magnitude; *gases expanding to a greater volume*"—(the "big bang" of creation?) may be the most fitting.

So was that what Bob had tried to tell me?

Once again an answer came from an unexpected source, confirming—more or less—the possibility of accuracy.

The March 20, 1994, issue of the *New York Times Book Review* shows on the front page, in broad headlines, this title: "THINGS ARE STRANGER THAN WE CAN IMAGINE." The subtitle says, "Two theoretical physicists think about them, in ten dimensions." It refers to two books, one by Kip S. Thorne, entitled *Black Holes and Time Warps: Einstein's Outrageous Legacy,* and the other is entitled *Hyperspace* by

Michio Kaku, subtitled *A Scientific Odyssey Through Parallel Universes, Time Warps, and the Tenth Dimension.*

Needless to say, I was overwhelmed. It was hard for me to comprehend most of it, but one part of the article stood out very clearly to me. The reviewer states: "Mr. Kaku believes that the mathematical theory of 'superstrings' may already have accomplished this" (that a "quantized theory of gravity would allow theorists to fit gravity into its proper place in the natural order of things") "by hypothesizing the existence of hyperspace. *In brief, this means thinking of reality in terms of ten dimensions,* rather than in terms of the three dimensions of space that ordinary mortals can perceive, plus the one dimension of time."

All of this intrigued me enough to try contact with Bob one more time—this time initiated by me for one more answer: I wanted him to tell me the other four dimensions. I can't say whether I really expected to get my answer—it was a spur-of-the-moment action. But the answer came!

It was brief and to the point: "Time, distance, mass, reaction," was all he said. I was overworked and tired at that time and put it aside to ponder.

I now had all ten dimensions.

"Space, speed, vision, balance, gravity, and sound" were the first six. Now "time, distance, mass, reaction" completed the cycle: *creation?*

Six years ago Bob had told me, a few months after his death, something I could hardly understand. Now, still not able to comprehend most of this, I can see that someone, somewhere, with the knowledge and ability was working on exactly the same thought process. Was my subconscious picking up some of these brainwaves from somewhere? But if that is possible, why should it not be possible that it *was* Bob who told me; one is as unusual as the other.

What I know for sure, though, is that it matters little what we, as human beings, know or do *not* know. What is, is, whether we are aware of it or not. But he presented me with another look at dimensional concepts known so far. He confirmed what I had suspected long ago. In the long run, everything of which we are part has a much simpler formula for existence than we think, and in the end it all comes back to *One*, the Alpha and the Omega: GOD, the Creator. The creation cannot be separated from its creator. All of us are part of one, again forming a total of one: *Unity*.

It had all started with the word *symphony*.

Now I know what the often-used phrase "symphony of life" means.

Every single person finds his or her own way of looking at life, at the world around, at the universe, at the workings of all things. My search for answers was prompted by curiosity, not by a need for proof.

What I found, makes me happy. It brightens my life and enriches it. It makes me cherish what is, will be, and has been.

But most of all, it makes me realize that we can all walk through the valley of the shadow of death, having to fear no evil, for the table is prepared before us.

What Is A.R.E.?

The Association for Research and Enlightenment, Inc. (A.R.E.®), is the international headquarters for the work of Edgar Cayce (1877-1945), who is considered the best-documented psychic of the twentieth century. Founded in 1931, the A.R.E. consists of a community of people from all walks of life and spiritual traditions, who have found meaningful and life-transformative insights from the readings of Edgar Cayce.

Although A.R.E. headquarters is located in Virginia Beach, Virginia—where visitors are always welcome—the A.R.E. community is a global network of individuals who offer conferences, educational activities, and fellowship around the world. People of every age are invited to participate in programs that focus on such topics as holistic health, dreams, reincarnation, ESP, the power of the mind, meditation, and personal spirituality.

In addition to study groups and various activities, the A.R.E. offers membership benefits and services, a bimonthly magazine, a newsletter, extracts from the Cayce readings, conferences, international tours, a massage school curriculum, an impressive volunteer network, a retreat-type camp for children and adults, and A.R.E. contacts around the world. A.R.E. also maintains an affiliation with Atlantic University, which offers a master's degree program in Transpersonal Studies.

For additional information about A.R.E. activities hosted near you, please contact:

A.R.E.
67th St. and Atlantic Ave.
P.O. Box 595
Virginia Beach, VA 23451-0595
(804) 428-3588

A.R.E. Press

A.R.E. Press is a publisher and distributor of books, audiotapes, and videos that offer guidance for a more fulfilling life. Our products are based on, or are compatible with, the concepts in the psychic readings of Edgar Cayce.

We especially seek to create products which carry forward the inspirational story of individuals who have made practical application of the Cayce legacy.

For a free catalog, please write to A.R.E. Press at the address below or call toll free 1-800-723-1112. For any other information, please call 804-428-3588.

A.R.E. Press
Sixty-Eighth & Atlantic Avenue
P.O. Box 656
Virginia Beach, VA 23451-0656